UP POHNPEI

PAUL WATSON was born in Lethbridge, Canada in 1984. He grew up in Bristol and studied Italian at the University of Leeds. After graduation he worked on Channel 4's Football Italia website, ran a satirical football website called Back of the Net and co-wrote a radio show for Radio Five Live, before leaving for Pohnpei. He lives in West London.

UP POHNPEI

A quest to reclaim the soul of football by leading
the world's ultimate underdogs to glory

Paul Watson

P

PROFILE BOOKS

First published in Great Britain in 2012 by
PROFILE BOOKS LTD
3A Exmouth House
Pine Street
Exmouth Market
London ECIR OJH
www.profilebooks.com

1 3 5 7 9 10 8 6 4 2

Typeset in Bembo by MacGuru Ltd
info@macguru.org.uk

Printed and bound in Great Britain by
Clays, Bungay, Suffolk

A CIP catalogue record for this book is available from the British Library.

ISBN 978 1 84668 501 9
eISBN 978 1 84765 800 5

For Lizzie and my parents

CONTENTS

We had to fly from London to Dubai, Dubai to Manila, Manila to Guam and finally Guam to Pohnpei with a forty-five-minute stop on the neighbouring island of Chuuk. Four flights and twenty-five hours in the air is a lot of time to think, but we made a valiant attempt to occupy our brains and prevent any doubts setting in. ❜

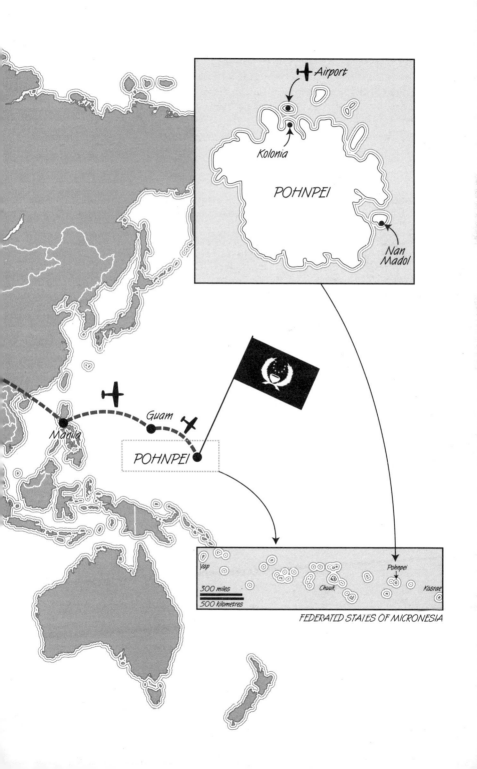

Airport

Kolonia

POHNPEI

Nan Madol

Guam

Manila

POHNPEI

Yap

Chuuk

Pohnpei

Kosrae

300 miles
500 kilometres

FEDERATED STATES OF MICRONESIA

PITCH IMPERFECT

'We have a problem with toads.'

I tried to blink away the sleepy haze from thirty-six hours of continuous travel to focus on the extremely skinny teenage boy in front of me. His name was Ryan and he'd been standing on his own when we arrived at the field, trying to do kick-ups with a slightly flat ball.

I had watched, fascinated, as he repeatedly flicked the ball up to head height and then, instead of heading it, at the last minute moved out of the way.

'Actually they have a problem with us,' he continued. 'This was their habitat and we built our football pitch on it. The toads have never really come to terms with it.'

'Ah,' I said, aware that I should sound authoritative. 'I see.'

I turned to Matt Conrad, my flatmate and partner in this expedition to Pohnpei, a tiny island in the central Pacific. He looked as though he was feeling equally off balance. In the incredible humidity, the short walk across the field had left us both soaked in sweat and his eyes were glassy with fatigue. Never, I thought, had conditions been less suitable for a ponytail. He made the smallest of gestures towards a shrug.

That explained why there were toads leaping all over the pitch, but why was there only one player?

A week before we arrived we had been cheerfully informed in an email that 'twenty players are turning up for practice regularly and can't wait for your arrival'. Then again, the email had been written by Edwin Sione, who ominously signed off as 'Pohnpei Soccer Coach'. Ominous because the sole reason we'd decided to abandon our lives in the UK and travel 8,000 miles around the world was that we'd been told there was a chance we would be able to coach football on the island. Things were going to be difficult enough, without having to depose someone from the job.

In the nervous weeks before our trip we had built up Sione into the key man we would have to deal with if we wanted to become involved in football on Pohnpei in any capacity. I imagined him as a brooding José Mourinhoesque figure, a tactical mastermind pacing the sideline, furiously protective of his patch. He had failed to pick us up at the airport as promised. On an island where just three flights arrive per week, I couldn't help thinking this was an early attempt at mind games. I found myself glancing nervously across the field, expecting him to appear at any moment.

But our guide, Charles (Char-Les to the islanders) Musana, was unflappable. He didn't seem the least bit concerned that the advertised 5 p.m. start time of our inaugural training session was easily half an hour behind us and just one footballer had so far come out of the woodwork.

'People here are on island time,' Charles chuckled, not a drop of sweat on his brow.

'If you say five p.m. here you mean six p.m. I reckon we'll have enough for a good game by seven.

'You have to remember that most local people here can't afford to own a car or even take a taxi. There's no bus service and the only bikes on the island are owned by the Mormons, so some of our players will be walking for an hour or longer just to get to training. In the day it's not too bad, but walking back at night you also have to deal with the dogs.'

There would be time to ask about the Mormons later, I reasoned. Unless they had mastered some form of drive-by conversion, they didn't seem to pose an immediate threat. As for the dogs, I had already noticed them in stray packs, lingering on street corners as we had driven here. Charles had warned us to expect some unwelcome attention from them in the evenings but cheerfully reassured us that Pohnpei was rabies-free.

I looked across PICS Field (the understandably commonplace acronym for 'Pacific Island Central School') and tried to imagine it as a fortress of football, a field of dreams.

Behind each semi-collapsed, netless goal, rolling hills of thick, shockingly green vegetation rose into the distance. Over the years the solitary stand had rotted under the continuous onslaught of one of the world's wettest climates. Puddles of that day's rainwater dotted the uneven pitch. It seems there weren't too many takers for the exhausting, thankless and expensive task of groundsman on an equatorial island.

At six o'clock the player count was still one. Including myself, Matt and Charles that made four of us.

'Well, we should definitely play a game of some kind,' said Matt.

'Yes,' I agreed wearily. 'Eight thousand miles for a game of two v. two. Great.'

It was made worse by the clear signs of life coming from the basketball court a few hundred metres away.

Always prone to fatalism, I had now become so sure that nobody would turn up that I was slow to notice the first players arrive. I turned round to find two identical men shaking hands with Charles. In my fragile mental state I feared I was hallucinating.

'Paul, these are the Paul brothers: Bob and Robert,' Charles offered by way of an explanation. I was greeted with the briefest of nods and a half-hearted handshake.

The two men quickly separated as Bob (or was it Robert?) went over to Ryan and gestured for the ball.

'Bob and Robert are twins,' said Charles, leaning in conspiratorially. 'They live in the same house but they can't stand each other.'

I nodded dumbly as the other twin walked a little way away and produced a small bag of lime powder, a leaf and a thumbnail-sized betel nut – the ingredients needed for an intoxicating chew. Almost every local we had met so far had been a betel-nut devotee, despite the habit's side effects of rotting teeth and stained red gums. The trade-off for such dismal oral hygiene was said to be an anaesthetic effect experienced as a numbing of the mouth that slowly progressed to the rest of the body. Although aware of the drug's ubiquity from my pre-trip research, I still couldn't help but feel slightly troubled at seeing people drive cars and operate heavy machinery unashamedly under the influence of this potent narcotic. Many Pohnpei pavements were stained metallic red by betel-nut juice, despite signs requesting pedestrians not to spit, although the more considerate chewers carried around beer cans for that purpose.

We now had three players, two of whom had my first name as their surname, looked identical and had variants on the same first name. I was trying to work out how I was ever going to distinguish between them when half a dozen or so other figures drifted across the field. I straightened my back, aware that any one of them could be Edwin Sione and desperate to look professional. Charles greeted the newcomers and introduced them to Matt and me for a handshake. It was hard not to feel like a member of the royal family at the FA Cup Final.

'This is Roger. I first taught him to play when he was six. He's walked all the way from Nett, which is miles away.'

Roger had long black hair pulled back in a ponytail. He bowed slightly as he shook my hand and backed away with a friendly grin.

Next in line were another set of brothers, Charles and Joseph Welson. Joseph was seventeen and allegedly had the hardest shot on the island, while Charles, four years Joseph's senior, was a goalkeeper.

Charles smiled at me. Joseph adopted more of a sneer. He didn't appear to have any teeth: another betel-nut fan.

'This is Rocky. He is a very athletic young man and he is one of the most dedicated players. Even when we aren't playing he comes and runs laps round the track.' Rocky offered us a facial expression somewhere between a grin and a scowl. After the briefest of nods he almost sprinted back to the other side of the pitch in a desperate attempt to avoid any small talk.

The introductions continued, coming thick and fast. I've never been particularly good at remembering names and my cause wasn't made any easier by the almost uniform haircut the players sported: one very long strand of hair running down their back, with the rest cut fairly short. This style, affectionately known as the 'rat tail', is seen almost as a status symbol, and takes years to grow. Like many seemingly Pohnpeian phenomena, the rat tail was borrowed from a mixture of outside cultures; the style had been very popular in Japan in the 1980s and Australia in the early 1990s and, while it had died out elsewhere, it had stuck in Pohnpei and become a badge of national identity. There's a story that one American basketball coach, an ex-military man, disapproved of the style and forced his players to shave off their rat tails. Many of the young lads went home in tears. The coach didn't last long after that.

After a lot of nodding and smiling, Matt and I explained we were going to have a practice game that evening. As I spoke, I realised that, rather than listening, most of the players were staring at Matt and me with open fascination. Matt sidled closer to me.

'It's the shorts, dude,' he said, stage-whispering out of the side of his mouth.

I looked at him blankly but he just tugged his shorts and looked meaningfully at me.

After a few moments, in which I thought the heat had sent him over the edge, I saw what he meant. Without exception the locals had opted for the long, baggy style of shorts – compared to them our shorter-than-knee-length versions must have looked like thongs.

Notwithstanding the baffled glances, we finally had the chance to give out some of the mountain of football equipment that we had brought with us. We handed out boots, socks, shin pads and the hard-won Yeovil Town and Norwich City shirts we had lugged halfway across the world.

The players pulled on their League One attire as if it were the most natural thing in the world, allowing Matt and me to breathe a sigh of relief that our trip hadn't been an inadvertent act of British football colonialism: a crusade by gung-ho football missionaries. It was almost inconceivable to us that anyone could not love football, but such creatures exist all over the world. What if we had found an island of people for whom the beautiful game held no appeal? A bag full of lower-league memorabilia couldn't solve that problem and would appear at best an act of misguided charity. Some players rejected the boots, preferring to play barefoot. Others had their own pairs that ranged in condition from coming apart at the seams to completely shredded.

The numbers had swelled, with more players introduced to us and more smiling and nodding until there were ten on each side. Matt and I lined up in midfield for opposing teams, hoping to establish the lie of the land while setting some sort of example.

Within minutes we could see that, although there was no shortage of enthusiasm, the game was a mess. One lad would get the ball and run ninety yards in a straight line before being brought down by one or more of a deep puddle, a toad and an opposition player, while another would boot the formerly white but now muddy brown ball off the pitch, over the stand and on to the road.

The players kept a safe distance from us, still openly sizing us up. Whenever Matt or I received the ball the opposition would give us a respectful five yards of space. There was no such treatment for Charles Musana, who was clearly a very talented player. One of the Paul twins (Robert, I think) clattered Charles before muttering an apology, offering his hand and charging off to find his next victim. He saved his worst foul for his brother Bob, who was goal hanging for the other team. A couple of seconds before Bob received the ball, Robert flew into him at waist height in something resembling a rugby tackle.

Players had no real idea what constituted a foul or how a pair of studded shoes and eighty yards of built-up momentum could damage another human. Tackles went flying in. Red-card challenges that would have sparked a full-team punch-up in an English Sunday League match were followed by a rueful smile and a slight wince.

There had clearly been precious little, if any, formal coaching on the island. But more than that, as most of them had never seen football on the television, the style of play was bizarre, bordering on alien. Even the least talented child playing football in a British park knows how to look like a footballer, how to spit, to raise their hands in despair at a poor pass or celebrate a goal with a clenched fist. There was none of that here.

I was shocked when the painfully polite Roger, who called me 'sir' when we were introduced, turned out to be the most ostentatious of the players, attempting the most spectacular of overhead kicks or diving volleys when a simple shot would have sufficed. Over the course of the match he performed enough acts of gymnastic brilliance to secure a medal at the Olympics, but he made little impression on the game. Nonetheless, a grin never left Roger's face, even when he was flattened by an opposition player or berated by a teammate.

We watched as, time and time again, our guide-to-toads Ryan would get himself into a good position, only to shrink back as another player came close: at one point he was perfectly placed to score a header but ducked out of the way at the last second, repeating the baffling technique we had seen him practising when we first arrived. Joseph proved why he was regarded as having the hardest shot on the island, scoring a thunderbolt of a goal, and when I'd whooped and clapped, he nodded and trotted back down the pitch, not even catching my eye.

My pre-trip reading on social norms in Micronesia had taught me that shouting orders, instructions or criticism is simply not done. Our guide Charles told us that if we reprimanded a player for anything, he would appear unfazed but would never show up again, unless we visited his family home and apologised. While it wasn't clear whether this had ever actually happened on the football pitch, there were plentiful stories of decades-long feuds caused by offences as minor as a spilt drink. In a tiny island community, the smallest perceived snub could be a fatal faux pas and being a rare foreigner in this environment meant that every action's significance was multiplied a hundredfold. It left Matt and me trailing around the pitch, calling out apologetically, trying desperately not to sound critical as we suggested to one of the players that perhaps it wasn't a good idea to run as fast as he could and slide head first into a player from twenty metres.

It didn't sound like a football game either. Every mistake was greeted by a howl of laughter from its perpetrator. The importance of saving face was so great that to miss a chance from six yards was unthinkable, whereas to intentionally sky the ball with the goal at your mercy was respectable. For a Pohnpeian, to try but fail is the ultimate embarrassment, but to try *to* fail is fine. The only vaguely recognisable feature was the mocking note in goalkeeper Charles Welson's voice after he made a one-on-one save or the grunt of disapproval from an unmarked striker watching a cross fly over the crossbar.

The odd contest was nearly an hour old when Charles Musana jogged up to me, tapped me on the shoulder and whispered 'Edwin Sione', nodding in the direction of a dark-haired man very deliberately lacing up his boots on the side of the pitch. My nemesis. I felt my throat tighten. I signalled to Matt, who was breathing hard, his hands on his knees, and he straightened to watch him too. This would be it, the moment of reckoning. Time seemed to slow as he pulled each lace tight and stood. He was disarmingly short, not much more than five feet, but I knew that what happened next would be key to the whole project.

I watched as the great man jogged on to the pitch. And then ran towards the ball clucking like a chicken and barking, 'Pass, pass to chicken man.' Within ten minutes, Sione had declared the goal-keeper to be offside and intentionally controlled the ball with his hand, arm and buttocks. I met Matt's eyes and could see him biting his lip trying not to laugh. We began to feel maybe we had over-estimated him.

We also began to wonder whether it was realistic to imagine anyone instilling order here. Although we tried to offer advice, there wasn't much of a sense that anyone was listening. Language was partly to blame for that. As an American protectorate, the official language of Pohnpei is English. However, it quickly became clear that locals were happier communicating in their native Pohn-peian. Despite being heavily influenced by the tongues of Pohn-pei's previous occupiers – English, Japanese, German and Spanish – the language somehow sounded completely alien. Sentences were punctuated with unfamiliar howling and clicking noises. Every now and again an English word would be used, followed by raucous laughter. It was a recipe for paranoia.

We were pretty sure as the game continued that the players were discussing us in detail and pretending not to understand us when it suited them. To make matters worse, our very English football vocabulary would probably not have been understood anywhere more exotic than Acton. References to bibs fell on deaf ears and a shout of 'man on' met with head scratching; even 'don't slide in with two feet' had to be abridged to 'don't kill him!'

We called time on our maiden game in Pohnpei once it became pitch black. Floodlights had once lit the field brightly, but now fewer than half a dozen functioning bulbs remained. Buying new ones from Japan had clearly never quite made its way to the top of the to-do list. Team Yeovil had come out as the resounding 8–4 victors, mostly thanks to Joseph's unstoppable right boot, although few of the goals would have stood had there been a qualified referee – and there certainly wouldn't have been many players left on the pitch.

The equipment was laboriously collected back in. Charles had advised us to do this at the end of every session, even though he had known the players for years. It wasn't that they would steal it, but in such a gerontocracy as Pohnpei, family elders could demand the possessions of younger relatives and etiquette demanded that they would never be able to ask for them back. Most families on Pohnpei don't own much, so any new items would be brought to the patriarch for examination, approval and possibly redistribution to another member of the family. The next we would see of our kit would be on a stranger wearing it while walking to the shops.

Rocky, clearly disappointed that the session was over, handed back his bib, nodded and walked away. Ryan folded his kit neatly and quietly wished us a pleasant evening. Bob and Robert succeeded in walking off with their boots on, but luckily Charles was on the ball and called Bob back just as he threatened to disappear into the night. Bob very slowly brought back the two pairs of shiny new boots, mumbling that he and his brother had been playing a prank on us. (When he left once more, Charles explained that to some degree Bob was telling the truth: he had expected to be caught, but that unchallenged he would very happily have worn the boots home.) Edwin Sione was conspicuous by his absence. He had skulked off when we started to collect the equipment in, leaving us to wonder exactly what he made of our arrival.

'So, what do you think?' asked Charles. 'Of course, there is also Ryan's cousin Dilshan. He's really good ...'

'Great!' This sounded promising.

'... but unfortunately, he is visiting his brother in Manila for the next three weeks.'

'Oh.'

A few other players mumbled a short, guttural phrase that I would later learn was 'pwong mwah' (good night) and then we were left alone in the field with hundreds of toads chirping in the darkness and thousands of unanswered questions – not least, what were we doing here in the first place?

'Still,' said Matt, 'at least it didn't rain.'

IN SEARCH OF THE LOST CAUSE

It began, as so many things do, with Andorra. In November 2007 Matt and I were sitting on the sofa, watching England lose their final Euro 2008 qualifying fixture to Croatia when, in the final minutes, the commentator uttered the immortal line: 'Of course, England will still go through if Andorra can beat Russia.'

To two football-obsessed men such as us, this was obviously insane.

Of course Andorra couldn't upset Russia! The tiny country, sandwiched between France and Spain, has a population of less than 84,000. In the just over a decade its national team had been in existence, they had played more than ninety games and only won three of them – and those had been against Albania, Belarus and Macedonia. Rather than hoping for an Andorran win, England would probably have been better off praying for Zeus to strike down Croatia's goalkeeper with a rogue thunderbolt. In fact, we reasoned, it was basically only the fact we hadn't been born in Andorra that was stopping Matt and me getting a game for them. Wasn't it? If we had been born in Andorra we would probably have racked up twenty or thirty international caps by this point in our lives. We'd be established international footballers.

You have to understand that Matt and I were particularly vulnerable to this type of thinking. We had met as students in Italy in 2006 and bonded there during that year's World Cup, of which we watched every single game. It was no small feat of endurance and pig-headedness. While others immersed themselves in Italian culture, we frequented dingy bar after dingy bar to roar on Costa Rica against Germany, Ecuador against Poland, and, most treacherously, everyone against Italy.

Back in the UK after graduating, I moved into Matt's spare room where, temporarily between jobs and bored to the point of insanity, he embarked upon a tireless programme of distraction. I was working from the flat as a football journalist specialising in Italian football, although Matt seemed determined to put a stop to that.

Aside from football, Matt's great passion was film, but finding a job in the industry had proven as hard as securing a contract with his beloved Tottenham Hotspur. He had applied to study film at the University of Southern California – one of the most respected courses in the world – but with so much competition for places, Matt had pretty much written off his chances of ever getting in, though he would still rifle through the post every morning just in case. He tried to keep his film-maker's eye in by pacing around the house with a hand-held video camera.

'You never know when something could happen,' he explained as I crunched my way through a bowl of Cheerios.

On one especially slow day Matt filmed me working for the best part of three hours, despite my vociferous protests. His resulting work – *Man Typing* – met with very little critical acclaim.

Matt's presence, plus the creeping feeling that I had covered every combination of events possible in a football season and was simply repeating them with different names, left me vulnerable to distraction. A game of 'Name that Norwegian Footballer' cost me three hours' work on one black Friday when Øyvind Leonhardsen's name inexplicably escaped me, while ranking every German team in order of how much we liked their kit compromised my writing sufficiently to warrant a severe talking to from my boss. (It was unquestionably worth it to establish that FC St Pauli, rather than Bayern Munich, were the powerhouse side of German football.) By the time we found ourselves sitting on that sofa, trying to work out which famous players we would have come up against if we had been playing for Andorra in our preferred positions over the last five years, this level of attention to detail had come to seem entirely normal.

In the end, of course, Andorra lost 1–0 to Russia. Even with all our bravado, we had to concede that any team Matt or I had ever represented would have struggled to hold Russia to a 1–0 deficit. But that night we started along a dangerous path. What about Lichtenstein or San Marino: surely we could play for them?

It probably goes without saying that I loved football. In truth I didn't really have any choice in the matter. As soon as I was able to walk, my impatient brother Mark thrust a football into my arms and told me it was my kick-off. In every childhood photo I am wearing a football shirt and so is Mark. The family photo albums could be mistaken for a chronology of Bristol City shirts in the 1980s and 1990s.

Football permeated every aspect of family life to the point where our exasperated mother had to ban discussion of the game during Sunday lunch; a ruling that we appealed against as passionately as a tough offside call. School friends supported Manchester United or Arsenal and changed allegiance at the slightest whim, sometimes several times during the same game. But already I didn't care about the glamour sides and glory hunting. It was the other end of the spectrum that fascinated me: the minnows. Instead of playing England v. Brazil in the garden, Mark and I conducted laborious qualification competitions with many a Saturday afternoon being sacrificed to Bolivia v. Paraguay or Saudi Arabia v. Yemen.

Inevitably, I dreamed of playing for my first love, Bristol City, and also for England, but two things were to stand in my way: a lack of any discernible natural talent and the professionalisation and globalisation of the sport. As a Tottenham Hotspur fan, Matt had set his sights a little higher but met with the same obstacles. He was as likely to become the new Gary Mabbutt as I was to be the next Dariusz Dziekanowski.*

When I was a kid, footballers were still, basically, normal people. The kind of men I could realistically aspire to be. Many of the players I saw on TV, and especially at Ashton Gate, were local lads, hard-working professionals grafting out a respectable living. It wasn't uncommon to see several moustaches, a comb-over or two and the odd player nursing a hangover on a Saturday afternoon. Maybe the players weren't riding the bus to games with the fans as they did in the 1920s, but most of them at least lived in the same city.

But somewhere in the 1990s, football changed. BSkyB brought

---

*A Polish striker who played for Bristol City 1992–3. He was hugely popular with fans at Ashton Gate but less so with the manager, whose wife he allegedly bedded.

huge money into the game after 1992, a trend accelerated by American entrepreneurs, oil-rich Arabs and Russian oligarchs, who started buying up clubs and adding to an ever-expanding influx of highly paid foreign stars. TV rights and merchandising quickly smothered a century of tradition. Ticket prices soared, leaving the average fan able to watch his team only whenever Sky deemed fit to broadcast their games while nouveau riche season-ticket holders filled the stands. Footballers were no longer mere employees: they were assets. And as such they had to be super athletes. The days of the captain handing out shots of whisky in the dressing room to prepare for a game were over. Maybe those scenes were best left behind along with Bovril and the Zenith Data Systems Trophy, but the link between those on the pitch and those in the stands very quickly eroded. There was no longer room for sentimentality and local boys made good.

Naturally I registered that the game I loved was changing before my eyes, but it still took a surprisingly long time to realise that I would never fulfil my dream of playing for England, or even Bristol City. Somehow I had never really taken stock of how far I had drifted from my boyhood aspiration until the night of England v. Croatia. I wrote about football for a living and played at weekends for an amateur side in London, where my performances ranged from forgettable to creditable. Although I had built a lifestyle that allowed me a substantial daily dose of the sport I loved, I wasn't ready to give up on my delusional football fantasies and felt thoroughly miserable at the compromise.

The day after the Croatia game, as the English media responded in typical measured fashion with apocalyptic headlines such as the *Sun*'s 'Useless, pathetic, insipid, spineless, desperate, rubbish: England are the joke of European football', and introduced an ingenious new moniker for manager Steve McClaren ('The Wally with the Brolly'), I was taking part in my own afternoon of football ignominy. My team was beaten, and beaten badly, by a fellow Ninth Division outfit in a Cup match on an ice-cold afternoon in Surrey. Worse still, I had travelled three and a half hours for the right to stand on the sidelines waiting to play just eight minutes when we were already six goals down and very much second best. I returned home, slamming the door shut, only to find Matt in even lower spirits.

'Tamworth!' he spat venomously.

'Excuse me?' I was pretty certain that greeting had never formally replaced 'Hello'.

'The Cape Verde Islands have got a goalkeeper, José Veiga, who plays for Tamworth in the Conference. There's no way we'd get in their team. I've tried Nepal, Belize, they're all too good,' Matt lamented, gesturing at both the computer screen and a stack of dirty plates, mugs and beer cans that bore testament to a misspent twelve hours.

By Monday, the search had reached a crisis point. I was desperately trying to write an article on the decline of Juventus for a looming deadline and ignored several yells of anguish from the next room, but a resounding crash fractured my fragile concentration. I tentatively peered into the living room where Matt, incandescent with rage, was glowering at his laptop, which had been knocked off the desk in the heat of the moment.

'Everything all right, mate?' I ventured.

'Tesfaye bloody Bramble. He plays for Stevenage Borough and Montserrat. It's over. Montserrat are the lowest team in the FIFA rankings and they're still too good.'

A few days earlier we had been convinced there was an

international team bad enough for us to represent them. Now it seemed that we were wrong. I began to reconcile myself to the idea I would never get a cap. I left Matt to it and got on with composing stinging indictments of Milan's transfer policy and profiles of players I'd barely heard of. My commitment to my job was fading. Every day I'd make up one ridiculous nickname for a player and see if anyone called me on it. Sometimes I'd nominate a day as an 'angry day' and have players 'lamenting', 'bewailing' and 'caterwauling' instead of the journalistic staple of 'stating'. Nobody ever noticed.

One rainy evening a few days later, I came back to the flat to find Matt glowing. He silently handed me a beer and opened his.

'Yap.'

I looked at him. 'Yap?'

'Yap.' He took a long swig from his beer and put it on the table carefully.

'There's another list.'

He was right. Though the FIFA World Rankings are meant to cover every team in the world, in reality they leave out many tiny islands, principalities, politically contentious territories and other places too poor, too small or too far away to be worth FIFA's while. These include Greenland, Monaco, Southern Cameroon, Lapland, Occitania and quite a number of others. In this parallel universe are islands without enough grass to mark out a pitch, teams so isolated they have nobody to play against and regions of disputed political status. Yet organised football is part of daily life for people in the incredibly remote British overseas territory of St Helena, the scarcely populated Easter Islands and the politically troubled regions of Iraqi Kurdistan and Tibet. There are even records of formal games on Antarctica between research scientists at weather stations. These are places where football had taken on common sense, and won. Matt grabbed me by the shoulders and steered me towards the computer, reading aloud the words on the screen. He was too excited to wait for me to read them myself.

'Yap is an island of 6,300 people in the Federated States of Micronesia, where stones are still used as currency alongside paper money.'

It might have a total population that would fit inside any football league ground in the UK, but Yap had a soccer association, with a proper badge, and a team that had recently lost 15–0 to Guam – not one of football's superpowers. I looked up at my grinning housemate.

'You've done it.'

He shook his head with a mixture of self-satisfaction and compassion. As he clicked to the bottom of the screen I saw in their list of past results a single win. Yap had once beaten one of their Micronesian neighbours: Pohnpei. Clicking through, the page for Pohnpei included a single sentence, which was enough to set my pulse racing:

'They have never registered a win, and are said to be the weakest football team in the world.'

I sat back in the chair. The search was over. If we couldn't play for Pohnpei, we couldn't play for anyone.

That night, we began learning about Pohnpei. As we read, the reasons for the island's poor football track record started to emerge. One of the four Federated States of Micronesia, Pohnpei is a Pacific island with a population of 34,000 – roughly the same as

Stroud in Gloucestershire. Two thousand miles north of Australia, the tiny island is one of the wettest places on earth and 91 per cent of its population is classed as medically overweight. This figure owes much to a diet strangely lacking in abundant local produce and heavily dominated by packaged, imported US tinned food.

We certainly weren't the first Europeans to happen upon Pohnpei. The Spanish occupied the island in the late nineteenth century before selling it to the Germans. The Germans subjugated the locals, who violently rose up in the Sokehs Rebellion of 1910, but were crushed. Eventually the Germans did leave when the island was given to Japan as part of their war reparations in the Treaty of Versailles. The US removed the Japanese at the end of the Second World War and the Micronesians have had a 'Compact of Free Association' with the US since 1989. The US hands over a size-able cheque to Micronesia each year to keep the region in its sphere of influence. In recent times, the Chinese have made subtle attempts to challenge American power by funding a large gym at the college and a grand new town hall. These 'friendship gestures' haven't gone unnoticed by the US, but are yet to convince the locals to switch allegiance.

Since other foreigners before us had managed to integrate into Pohnpeian society, we could see no reason we couldn't do the same. There would, of course, still be the small issue of citizenship, but anyone who'd watched Welsh captain Vinnie Jones (who famously admitted to only having been to Wales two or three times), standing in bemused silence as the Welsh national anthem played, knew there were ways around such things. For now, we had somewhere to start.

The Pohnpei Soccer Association had a website and even a list of contact email addresses, but the page hadn't been updated for five years. We composed a calm email stating our 'interest in football in the region' and desire to 'find out more', deciding not to play all our cards at this stage. In any case, we didn't hold out too much hope of a reply. At first our negativity seemed to be well founded as emails came flying back as undelivered. But a few days later we had a reply – from a Charles Musana. Charles was the vice-president of the Pohnpei Soccer Association and he sent us a very polite message thanking us for our interest in the game in Micronesia. However, it was very hard to concentrate on much of what he wrote as I had already skipped ahead after catching sight of the sentence, 'My family is moving to London in December.'

It was 26 November; Mr Musana would be in England in just over a fortnight's time. We rubbed our eyes, re-read the email and then arranged to meet him in Piccadilly Circus on his second day in the country. Slightly shocked by the speed at which fantasy had moved closer to reality, I felt it was time to discuss the idea of playing international football for Pohnpei with my family. I decided that if anyone would understand my motives, it would be my brother. Mark was captivated by the story so far and immediately began his own line of research. Hours later I received an email with the subject line: Micronesian Naturalisation. The body text read simply: 'There may be a few problems with this bit, mate.' Attached was a document from the Federated States of Micronesia Government website, listing the requirements for naturalisation.

§ 204. Naturalisation.

The President may naturalise a person as a citizen of the Federated States of Micronesia in a manner or form prescribed by law or regulation if the person:

(1) shall have lawfully resided within the Federated States of
    Micronesia, for at least five years;
(2) is a child or spouse of a citizen or is a national of the
    Federated States of Micronesia;
(3) upon naturalisation, shall have renounced previous citizenship
    and allegiance to any and all foreign powers and rulers, and
    taken an oath of allegiance; and
(4) has competence in at least one of the indigenous languages of
    the Federated States of Micronesia.

Vinnie Jones may have been able to play for Wales but he
wouldn't be able to play for Pohnpei. Reluctant to give up without
a fight, I began to weigh up the difficulty of the quest. I had
studied languages at university and although a Micronesian tongue
would be more challenging than Italian, I felt I could probably
cross the language barrier. But that was the tip of the iceberg.
Could I really live in Pohnpei for five years? Would I sacrifice my
British passport to play international football? I decided against
asking my girlfriend Lizzie whether there was any room for nego-
tiation on marrying a Pohnpeian woman. Eventually, I admitted
defeat. The sense of deflation was enormous – but nonetheless, we
weren't going to stand up Charles Musana.

As Matt and I waited at Piccadilly Circus on the coldest night in
many years we wondered why we had chosen to meet anyone in
Piccadilly Circus and how we would recognise a man we had never
seen.

'So how sure are we that this is a wind-up?' Matt asked, stamping his feet as we scanned the faces of the people walking past.

'About ninety per cent, I reckon.'

Although we had looked at pictures of Pohnpei natives on the internet, we still weren't really sure what he would look like, so we took to smiling hopefully at anyone who looked vaguely equatorial. Several tourists quickened their pace when they caught our eye. After five minutes of fruitless standing and smiling, Matt had clearly had enough. 'I say we look for the coldest man.'

Over by the fountain, we found a tall man and a woman looking bemused and chilled to the bone. He smiled when he saw us approaching. 'Oh, good,' said Charles. 'I thought it was a prank.'

Moving quickly to prevent hypothermia, we whisked the Musanas off to a curry house and quizzed them about all things Pohnpeian. The first thing we learned was that Charles was not born in Pohnpei but actually travelled to the island from Uganda. He had left for the US and eventually wound up in Pohnpei teaching business at the College of Micronesia after chancing upon an advert online. Charles was a born football lover, and had spent many years trying to stimulate the growth of football on the island with varying degrees of success. Every day without fail he would make a significant drive after work to go and play football for his team, the Local Warriors. His wife Lydia would have had reason enough to be upset, except that she also loved the game and played too.

Though we had only really met Charles out of politeness, having decided in light of my brother's findings that there was no way we would ever be able to play international football for Pohnpei, we became genuinely fascinated by what he told us about the island. After a brief period of funding around the millennium, football there had been largely ignored by the powers that be and was reduced to a series of games between the island's locals and assorted foreigners, contested on a pitch that was barely playable. Occasional grudge matches against passing French navy ships or the US Coastguard were the highlights in the football calendar. It was a bruising encounter every time the French navy turned up, Charles recalled with a grin. He told us the story of the last meeting between the two teams when the Pohnpei side had been duped by the Frenchmen. The sailors had kindly invited their opposite numbers to come aboard for a meal the night before the game. Once there, they plied them with a torrent of alcohol. The next day, a worse-for-wear Pohnpei side were surprised not to recognise most of the opposing team. They had very wisely got an early night, leaving the Pohnpeians to drink themselves into oblivion with their non-footballing colleagues.

A very pleasant yet ultimately unfulfilling evening was drawing to a close when Charles uttered the sentence that stopped us in our tracks.

'A couple of us would help to teach the kids but the biggest problem for football in Pohnpei is that there isn't a coach as such.'

I stopped mid-naan and looked over to Matt: the significance of Charles's statement hadn't been lost on him either. At the same time as it occurred to me, I could see the wheels turning in his head. As Englishmen, we might never be able to *play* for Pohnpei, but there was certainly no reason we couldn't coach there. There was the minor drawback that neither of us had a single coaching qualification to our name, but how hard could it be?

We left the Musanas shivering outside the restaurant, after telling Charles we'd keep in touch. Although he hadn't said it outright, he had clearly been dangling the idea of coaching football on Pohnpei in front of us. He'd been very clear that there would be no money, either for equipment or for us, and that football was in a terrible state there, with no funding or sponsorship – there wasn't even a league of teams to select a Pohnpei side from. There was an absolute lack of direction. But to us, that just made the proposition all the more attractive. We could start with a completely clean slate. Though neither of us would admit it, our current state of disillusionment with the scale, pomp and privilege of modern European football added an element of idealism to excitement. We were going to make a difference.

As England raced towards Christmas, some days the idea was brilliant, other days it seemed ridiculous. Why would any sane person leave a secure job and a comfortable flat for a remote, rainy island they had never visited? I could see all the reasons it would be incredibly difficult. In England, football is so woven into our culture that it's impossible to get away from, even if you're one of the many people who want to. Games blare out from the doorways of pubs, newspapers devote pages and pages to transfer rumours, radio phone-in shows clog up the airwaves with fans having their say. On Pohnpei, there would be none of that. First of all, we would need to create a league, so that there were enough players capable of lasting ninety minutes of football to choose the best of them for the national team. But even that was getting ahead of ourselves. Before we could create a league we would need kit – balls, boots, shirts and at least one playable pitch. We were far from sure we could count on even these basics.

On the other hand, why would anyone turn down the chance to manage an international football team? Pohnpei had taken root in my consciousness and refused to leave without a fight, so I turned to the only person who could help me settle this once and for all: my girlfriend Lizzie. She had always been remarkably tolerant of my love of football and I had always been equally tolerant of her lack of any interest in it. In fact, like any addict, I had tried to shelter her from my vice.

'I think you should do it.'

It was the one response I hadn't been prepared for.

'You've just said that it's what you want to do. It's your childhood dream. If you don't try, then you'll always regret it.'

I found myself fighting the corner of rationality, unexpectedly playing devil's advocate. 'I won't earn any money. It's going to cost me two thousand pounds just to get there. I'll end up in so much debt …'

'Well, it's not like they pay you much at the moment. And you hate your job.'

'I'm going to be on the other side of the world for weeks on end.'

'Yes, but if you were here you would be wishing you were there, wouldn't you? I'd rather you were there wishing you were here. You should at least go and see what it's like.'

Christmas came and went and still I prevaricated. It was February 2008 and Matt and I had spent three months laboriously weighing up the pros and cons. It was time for me to make up my mind.

'So, we're going, then, aren't we?' I said decisively to Matt one morning.

'Of course we're going,' he said with an air of strained patience. 'It's not like I've got anything else to do.'

'What about your family? Won't they try to talk you out of it?'

'Talk me out of it? My parents would drive me to Pohnpei if they could. You've only lived with me for a month or two, they've had twenty years.'

We were going to do it, but we would need time to find the

money. We pencilled in July 2009 as our departure date. Charles Musana had told us that he planned to return to Pohnpei then and had volunteered to show us round and introduce us to everyone who mattered in the island's football community. We knew that could make a huge difference to our chances of success.

Although we had a whole seventeen months to prepare, there was plenty of preparing to do. Once we had made the decision to go for it there was an endless string of things that needed taking care of. Though nominally a fact-finding exercise, our visit would be essentially a job interview. We knew that while we were checking out the island, everyone involved would be checking us out, too. Though it didn't seem like the most formal place to work, there would be all sorts of people we'd need to impress, not least the players. The new England manager Fabio Capello had just arrived in London having won trophies everywhere he'd coached – his list of honours was as long as the phone book. We brought only our enthusiasm and a disturbingly broad knowledge of international football trivia.

We had to take Pohnpei by storm, arrive on a wave of positivity to show the players we meant business and to get them excited. We sent an email to Charles to tell him the 'fact-finding mission' was definitely on and then sat back grinning. We began the elaborate process of planning how we would go about reinvigorating football on Pohnpei. I was still training with an amateur team in West London, but suddenly my focus changed from polishing up my playing skills to learning the ropes of coaching. Although my team was a world away from professional, we had a talented coach who had played in Italy's top divisions. I stopped mindlessly doing drills and for the first time began to question what they were achieving. After each session I would come home and make illustrated notes of the exercises we had done. I was the first to arrive at training and the last to leave. In my spare time I studied the tactics, physiology and psychology of football harder than I had ever studied academically. I read everything I could that might prepare me for the world of the coach.

Still unsure whether our coaching knowledge would hold up, we turned attention to the issue of equipment. If we turned up with bags of kit it would surely make us look professional and get us off on the right foot. Charles had told us that the players were lacking all types of equipment but it was mostly shirts and boots that they needed. And so one Sunday afternoon, I sat down and composed emails to the ninety-two professional clubs in England, begging for donations to a good cause. It was agonisingly slow work.

Dear ...

At the start of May I took control of the Football Association of the Federated States of Micronesia.

My objective is to rejuvenate football in a region where the game is still in its infancy and the first step is the formation of an organised League, which will commence in September 2009.

The major obstacle that we face is a lack of equipment and that is why I am approaching your club. In the forthcoming League there will be six teams, each needing their own kit, and we would like these to be provided by six English clubs. We would like (CLUB NAME) to be one of those clubs.

Your support would be an invaluable boost for football in Micronesia. It would also raise the profile of (CLUB NAME/NICKNAME), giving the club a greater global presence with the shirts being pictured in newspapers and online.

I would very much appreciate the chance to discuss the project and will happily address any questions you may have.

It wasn't a bad email. However, there were a few possible stumbling blocks – the main one being that we weren't in charge of the Federated States of Micronesia Football Association; I hadn't even been there. I also wondered how much trust clubs would place in an email sent from a Hotmail account by a British man asking for kit for a country they had never heard of. In most people's eyes, I was probably one rung up from a Nigerian billionaire looking for a short-term loan. Still, nothing was ever achieved without a few white lies – but even as I clicked Send on the ninety-second email I braced myself for ninety-two refusals.

Amazingly, the first 'no' came from Bristol City – the club I had supported from birth. In their email I had stressed my link to City but this was the response, strangely, written in blue, the colour of City's local rivals, Bristol Rovers:

Dear Paul,
Whilst I appreciate that you are a lifelong supporter of the club, we are still not able to assist with your request.
    Good luck with sourcing your items, perhaps someone would be interested in sponsoring you.

And there it was, the answer from a team I had pumped literally thousands of pounds into over the last twenty-four years. What chance did I have with the likes of Swindon, Huddersfield or, dare I say, Bristol Rovers?

Having contacted every club in Britain – even those with less money than I had – I played the waiting game for several days.

Over the coming weeks, Shrewsbury and Sheffield United flirted, saying they'd like to be involved but would need to know more about the project. We were close, but couldn't seal the deal. Then came a call from Yeovil Town community department head Dave Linney offering us a set of last season's shirts. I gratefully accepted, hung up and then danced round the room. We had sixteen pretty green and white shirts to hand out. Matt felt very confident.

'You watch. Now we've got Yeovil on board, the other clubs will fall like dominoes.'

A week went by without a single email.

'Well, maybe dominoes isn't quite the right word.'

Newly relegated Norwich City certainly wanted in on the act and sent us over a heap of outdated shirts. Some of them had been personalised with names like 'Deano' and 'JJ' but we weren't going to look a gift-horse in the mouth. We'd just have to give the players in Pohnpei British-sounding nicknames at a very early stage.

The Premier League clubs remained elusive. There was no reply from the bloated superpowers, but Hull City were at least kind enough to let us know that they were not at all interested in helping us. Then there was an email from Tottenham. As a huge Spurs fan, Matt had been determined to secure some shirts from White Hart Lane and when I told him the email had come through, he bounced round the room with a look of elation on his face.

'Vindication!' he boomed.

Then I explained that they were saying we could buy sixteen of last year's shirts for the reduced rate of £20 each. We soon worked out that this wasn't fantastic value, especially given that they were retailing for £25 in the club shop and about £15 in Lillywhites. Matt sat on the sofa, muttering to himself.

'Eleven million for Sergei Rebrov, sixteen million for Darren Bent, sixteen million for David Bentley? And *we* have to pay *them*?'

After twelve emails, I had used all my business acumen to negotiate £15 per shirt. The money would have to come from our own pockets. It was a big decision to make as we also needed to have enough to buy boots to take over, but the chance to have a Premier League team behind us proved too good to refuse.

Knowing that I would have to support myself for a while with no income, even if just for our first trip, I was trying to fit in all of the research and fundraising around my job and when I wasn't working or trying to scrounge football shirts, I was at the gym. We didn't have enough time to improve our skill level noticeably before we arrived in Pohnpei, but I could at least ensure that I was fit. Over the course of the next year, we planned and saved as much as possible. There were very few books on Pohnpei, but we read everything that was available, desperate to be as well prepared as we could be. Charles was now living in London, and we stayed in regular contact with him. He was supportive throughout, and told us what we could expect to find when we arrived. I was astonished when another Christmas came and went. There was just half a year to go, but it seemed as if things were gradually reaching the stage where we'd be ready to head out to Pohnpei.

Once I'd handed in my notice in February 2009 it became very hard to keep working. I was still expected to do fourteen-hour days but working at home afforded me certain opportunities. I would run two miles to get to the gym and sprint back after a session hoping nobody in the office would have tried to contact me during my absence.

I slept poorly and had nightmares that everything would fall through – what if someone else came up with the same idea and got there first? I wouldn't even mention Pohnpei to close friends in case the next time they called it was from a football pitch in Micronesia. If I couldn't get hold of Charles Musana for a day I would panic, presuming that our only link to Pohnpei had backed out. When Charles stopped answering my calls for three weeks, I was a wreck. He chuckled when he returned to Chingford to find twelve increasingly panicked voicemail messages.

'Maybe I should have told you I was going to Uganda to see my family,' he said. 'I hope I didn't worry you.'

I tried to convince Charles I wasn't a stalker but felt embarrassed that a man I barely knew had felt it necessary to apologise for visiting his parents without consulting me. I resolved to stop fearing the worst.

My final day as a football journalist was an anticlimax. After months of anticipation, 5.30 p.m. came and that was that. Working at home certainly took away any sense of occasion and I genuinely regretted not going through with my plan of drinking myself into a stupor while typing increasingly libellous stories. Although I knew that in the long term I had taken a huge step towards making the Pohnpei move a reality, in the short term I had just thrown in my job during one of the worst economic slumps in living memory. I had saved some money, but certainly not as much as I had hoped, especially if I was going to work on a voluntary basis in Pohnpei for the foreseeable future.

As departure day loomed, Matt and I scurried around looking for bargain boots, balls and shin pads, eating further still into our modest savings. Then there were the medical precautions. I had to pay over £100 for a massive array of immunisations, which was a particularly galling experience, given my embarrassing phobia of needles.

On 18 July 2009 at 8 p.m., we were packed and ready to go. On 18 July 2009 at 8.05 p.m., in a bid to save money on excess luggage, we unpacked our bags and removed all packaging and labelling. Three hours later and eleven grams lighter, we gave up and went to bed. It had been just under two years since we had taken our first steps and now we were going to Pohnpei.

As 19 July dawned, neither of us had slept. The journey to Heathrow was a quiet one as we both spent it wondering exactly what we had got ourselves into.

2
MONEY FOR NOTHING

It was the morning after our first kickabout on the PICS Field, and as I sheltered from torrential rain in the doorway of a small grocery shop, I noticed the cashiers exchanging the sort of grin reserved for foolish foreigners.

'Rainy season,' said the rat-tailed boy at the closest till.

I watched water gushing from the roof, leaking down the side of the shop and churning up mud. I nodded, determined to seem unimpressed.

'So, when does it start?' I asked casually as if I knew but had temporarily forgotten.

He looked at me quizzically for a moment, lazily flicking his betel nut from cheek to cheek.

'January,' he said.

'And when does it end?'

The cashiers turned away with a slight grin.

'December.'

I ran back to the hotel, where I found Matt wincing, unpacking Vaseline, baby oil, hydrocortisone cream and talcum powder.

'Arse chaffage,' he said matter-of-factly, waving his hand in the air. 'It's the humidity.' He walked carefully towards the bathroom. 'I feel like I've had a one-night stand with Seabiscuit.'

I tried to offer my deepest sympathy, but Matt shrugged it off. I sat on the bed and started to psych myself up. It was our first full morning on the island and we were due to meet with Jim Tobin, the secretary general of the Federated States of Micronesia National Olympic Committee. There was no way we'd be able to coach on Pohnpei without his approval.

The sovereign island nations that make up the Federated States of Micronesia (FSM) had a chequered sporting history. Surveying the sorry conditions at PICS Field at practice the night before, Charles had explained that the facilities had been gleaming and spotless nearly a decade ago, when athletes from the four FSM islands attended the Micronesian Games. Pohnpei competed against neighbours Yap, Chuuk and Kosrae, as well as other countries in the region, in an odd assortment of track and field events and traditional contests including spear fishing and coconut shaving. With Micronesia spanning over a million square miles of ocean (Pohnpei and Yap are nearly 2,000 miles apart), these events are a big deal. Thousands of excited locals had flocked to the events and cheered on their heroes to an impressive haul of medals. Now, the running track was uneven and full of holes, the seating area eroded, the ceremonial statue that held the Games torch was used as a makeshift toilet and, most pertinently for us, the football field resembled a wetlands reserve.

Jim's office was a short walk from the hotel, on the third floor of a building shared with the Red Cross. By the time we got there we were out of breath and sweating. We'd both put on jeans for the meeting as a nod to formality but my legs were clammy and damp and I could already confidently predict that denim wasn't going to be a significant component of my island wardrobe. Up a stairwell, the Micronesian Olympic Committee logo, which looks like a

Christmas pudding, proudly told us we had reached our destination. The walls were covered in yellowing newspapers detailing the modest past glories of Micronesian athletes, amongst which a painting depicting the Micronesian team at the Sydney Olympics in 2000 hung in pride of place. Charles knocked on the door marked 'FSM NOC' and we entered the inner sanctum of Micronesian sport: a modestly sized room with three desks and pigeonholes for mail dedicated to each of the sports. The slot marked 'soccer' was worryingly empty. Various souvenirs from past Olympics were strewn across the floor and balanced precariously on shelves.

Like every other nation, Micronesia has representation at the Olympics. As with many small states, a handful of FSM athletes are allowed to enter events in a 'wild card' capacity, skipping the qualification process to be thrown straight in at the deep end. In 2000, Pohnpeian Elias Rodriguez ran in the marathon, qualifying automatically although nobody outside the island had ever seen him in action. Needless to say, he was hopelessly underprepared. He had never run the full distance, had nobody to train with or against and could hardly run twenty-six miles on Pohnpei without running into the ocean.

Rodriguez came dead last – eighty-first out of the eighty-one athletes who finished the race – but was a national hero nonetheless. His photograph was all over the walls. When we asked several locals what Elias was doing these days, we had been met with bemused stares and shrugs. Eventually a stern police officer told us the Olympian was 'working up by the airport' but warned us that Rodriguez had quit running almost overnight three years ago and gently hinted that he may not relish the chance to discuss why with two strange white men.

Representing such a minnow nation certainly hadn't disillusioned Jim Tobin. Jim had come to Pohnpei as a short-term volunteer with the Peace Corps but had fallen in love with a Micronesian woman and settled down to have a family. These days the locals considered him Pohnpeian and so did he. As we entered his office, the towering American bounded up to greet us with a powerful handshake.

'Matt, Paul, great to meet you. Any friend of Charles is a friend of mine.'

Charles had worked with Jim throughout his fifteen years on the island, during which time football's fortunes had risen and fallen: in the late 1990s a FSM team had been formed, based in another of the four constituent states, Yap. The aim was to unite the quartet, who had been competing against each other for a few years, in one official national team, rather like Great Britain at the London Olympics. The team had managed to lure a respected Israeli coach called Shimon Shenhar and travelled to Fiji for the South Pacific Games in 2003. Shenhar was actually 'given' to Micronesia by the Israeli government as a sign of gratitude for the strange political alliance between the two nations: Israel was one of the first countries to establish diplomatic relations with the Federated States of Micronesia and since then, in any international forum, Israel can count on the Micronesian vote. In their first international outing, the Micronesians were outclassed and lost 17–0 and 16–0 to much longer established, if not internationally renowned, sides New Caledonia and Tahiti. These nations had taken 15–0 humiliations of their own against the likes of Australia and New Zealand but had stayed the course and relished the chance to deal out some punishment.

Rather than see the tour as a building block, the government and the sports councils saw it as an expensive failure. Funding was removed, Shenhar left and the game became moribund. Obesity was already endemic throughout the island, largely due to poor diet and a lack of options for exercise, and several of the 'stars' of the Micronesian squad had sought comfort in junk food and recreational drugs. We had come to Pohnpei in the hope of being the leaders of the next footballing generation and to prevent another wave of promising athletes from losing heart and gaining weight.

We had expected Jim to grill us on our credentials. We had none, a short stint in England's basement divisions and some Sunday League glory aside. Matt, who rarely looks fazed, was shifting in his seat and sweating and I was sure that nerves were to blame rather than chaffage. But the softly spoken Montana native was a steam train of enthusiasm, ready to tell us everything we wanted to hear. I'd rehearsed the conversation fifty times on the journey to Pohnpei and it had never gone so well. Edwin Sione didn't coach Pohnpei's football team, Jim immediately reassured us. He was a wrestling coach at the college, who occasionally turned up at PICS Field. For a brief and baffling period, Sione had tried to merge wrestling and football into a bizarre combi-sport. The result was widespread confusion.

'I stuck my neck out for soccer during the Shenhar regime because I really thought, I still do think, it's the best sport for Micronesia,' Jim said. 'I thought we could follow the example of Guam, where things have really taken off. Now look at them climbing the FIFA World Rankings.'

In most things, it seemed, Guam acted as a big brother to Pohnpei. While Pohnpei is an American protectorate, Guam is a US territory outright and looks like a scaled-down version of Reno. Most Pohnpeians seemed in awe of the bright lights of

Guam with its shiny shopping malls, two-lane highways and bustling nightlife.

'But as soon as he left, we had nobody to take his place and people told me I should have stuck with individual sports like athletics. There's this general belief here that Pohnpeians can't make successful sports teams.'

He declared that what Pohnpei needed was a full-time, dedicated football coach. What Pohnpei needed was someone to train the youth and build a state team. What Pohnpei needed was us.

'I can smell bullshit from a mile away but you guys are genuine. You've funded yourselves to come out here for this taster. If you can get back here then the job is yours. There's no money for a salary but I'll support you in any way I can. If we can get some momentum going, then maybe we can revisit that.'

I looked at the clock. Just twenty minutes had passed but everything had changed. All we had done to qualify was fly across the world. We could have gone home, altered Wikipedia and gone back to our normal lives with a decent dinner-party story, but we both knew that was never an option. We were officially the new coaches of Pohnpei's football team.

'Look, I'm not saying it's completely unexpected. Anyone who bases life decisions on information found on Wikipedia deserves everything they get.'

Matt was pacing about the hotel room, waving a piece of paper about to punctuate what he was saying. 'If they don't actually accept pebbles here, we're screwed. They want eighty-seven dollars for those fliers.' I misguidedly tried to calm Matt down by pointing out that we had possibly overdone the flier order – 1,000 would be enough to tile the entire island and we had only found a handful of places a flier could be posted where it wouldn't immediately be destroyed by the rain.

'It's not just the fliers, Paul. Have you been in a shop? It's all so bloody expensive. Everything is imported, so everything is rare. Do you know what they charge for an apple? A fiver! I just want the minutes to record the fact that our economic model for the trip is going to have to be radically altered if, as appears likely, the option to pay in shale is taken off the table.'

Five days into our three-week scouting mission and we were beginning to see the scale of the task in front of us. Although I knew that Matt wasn't really furious about the price of an apple, he was absolutely right that things were very different from how we'd imagined they would be. Our optimism after the inaugural Pohnpei kickabout just hours after we landed already seemed ancient history. On the outbound journey we had done everything we could to avoid facing the reality of spending every penny we had on what was literally a flight of fancy. It had cost the best part of £2,000 to get to Pohnpei and it wasn't hard to see why. We had to fly from London to Dubai, Dubai to Manila, Manila to Guam and finally Guam to Pohnpei with a forty-five-minute stop on the neighbouring island of Chuuk. Four flights and twenty-five hours in the air is a lot of time to think, but we made a valiant attempt to occupy our brains and prevent any doubts setting in.

I had fraudulently declared myself to be Britain's fifth best Battleships player. Matt found me out by winning three consecutive games against me on the in-flight entertainment system. The sting of defeat psyched me up to win forty straight games of Pong – a glorious reign that lasted for the best part of three hours and caused great entertainment in Seats 22a and 22b but was less popular with the rest of the plane. Matt was so dejected by defeat thirty that he challenged and ruthlessly beat an eight-year-old girl who was sitting opposite us. Charles had been on the same flight. He'd wisely managed to avoid the indignity of sitting in our row but was close enough to hear the ups and downs of in-flight computer battle and wore the tired look of a man realising he had left his young children at home only to babysit two twenty-five-year-olds. But as we got further from home, we became more and more nervous. For the arduous Manila–Guam leg, the airline seemed to show mercy on poor Charles and upgraded him to first class. Battling extreme tiredness and fuelled by nervous energy, we took it in turns to annoy the other. As Matt flagged, I would perk up. When I just needed to be left alone he would suddenly decide to quiz me on the capital cities of Africa.

The excitement of that journey seemed far behind us now as we paced our modest quarters in Pohnpei. Our childlike enthusiasm had been replaced by a middle-aged air of resignation. We had managed to organise a couple of workouts, but only a few of the players who had shown up the first time had come back and the long evenings at PICS Field ended up being more kickabouts than training sessions. We handed out the equipment and we gathered it in again, but we still weren't really in charge and our grip on proceedings felt very precarious. Any attempt to run a training drill as opposed to the largely formless games the players were used to would have risked destroying the very tentative relationships we had so far established. We simply tried to regulate the chaos by slowly phasing in more and more of the rules of the game, picking up on handballs, career-ending tackles and the occasional ten-yard offside.

The only people who seemed to turn up regularly were the players who belonged to the rather grandly named International FC – a group of non-native Pohnpeians who got together for matches every so often. We knew we had to do something drastic if our first trip wasn't going to be the most expensive park kick-about in history. As well as the fliers, Matt had come up with the idea of a television commercial, saying, 'JFK proved that to spread your message successfully, you have to reach the people through television.' Charles had arranged for us to have a meeting with someone he knew at the television station but we didn't hold out much hope that a commercial would make any difference, and found our enthusiasm dwindling day by day. It was partly the weather. After a week of never quite drying out before braving the next downpour, I realised that I hadn't been prepared for what it actually meant to live in what some sources claimed to be the third wettest place on earth. Maybe it was because I'm never that impressed at being the third best at anything (with the possible exception of Battleships) – or more likely it was because I'm a typical Brit and I like to think I know a thing or two about rain. In Pohnpei, however, the average rainfall is more than ten times that of Manchester. It rains more or less every day and when it does you feel like the world is ending.

To stave off the boredom when we were cooped up, Matt and I had invented and become aficionados of a game we played in our hotel room using a screwed-up cigarette packet and two carrier bags. Although we spent hours drafting a complex series of rules and a code of sportsmanship, to the untrained eye it would have looked a lot like two men fighting and occasionally throwing a ball of plastic into a bag. On the day of the flier debacle we decided that we had to actually leave the hotel room to let off some steam, but we were forced to cancel our plans to travel round the island when the roads flash-flooded, and we resigned ourselves to spending long periods sheltering in the nearby Palm Terrace shopping centre. (To call Palm Terrace a shopping centre is to flatter it a little – it's a department store selling groceries and local handicrafts at hugely inflated prices and various assorted kitchen items at astronomical ones. The selection of items, as with all other shops on the island, resembled a *Generation Game* conveyor belt. Spam and stationery shared an aisle while a pool table sat in the corner next to a rack of machetes, some trainers and a paddling pool as though it were the most natural thing in the world. And like many other buildings in Pohnpei the exterior had seen better days, the sign on the roof forlornly declaring 'PALM ★ T RR CE'.)

Just as we prepared to bunker down for the morning, the rain stopped. Within seconds the sky turned from end-of-the-world black to a deep blue, and scorching sunshine immediately set about the considerable task of drying up the puddles. Matt and I deliberated at length whether the road would be too treacherous and whether the rain would start up again but we were interrupted by Charles, who pulled up alongside us in our rental car. 'If you wait for the weather to clear up you'll never do anything in Pohnpei. Let's show you some of the island,' he said. The voice of experience had spoken.

Charles drove us out of the capital Kolonia and into the island proper, dodging deep potholes every ten yards and swerving to avoid lethargic dogs. We passed the rotted grey of Pohnpei State Hospital and its privately owned rival, the garish pink surgery Genesis, and the jungle beckoned ahead like a scene from *Jurassic Park*. Matt was leaning further and further out of the window filming both the scenery and bemused locals with a hand-held camera. William Blake famously described England as a 'green and pleasant land', but he hadn't visited Pohnpei as far as I know. The combination of daily deluge and constant sunlight gave the island a climate like an open-air greenhouse and everywhere we looked nature was vying for space with mankind. The houses became more ramshackle as we left Kolonia, often dwarfed by larger communal huts that were designed for drinking sakau. Made from the root of hibiscus plants, sakau, like betel nut, is a local mind-altering drug. Also like betel, the sticky brown mud-like substance is a soporific, lulling the drinker into a sleepy stupor. Sakau is at the centre of many island ceremonies and crucial to any self-respecting Pohnpeian's night out.

As if under its influence, everyone we drove past seemed to be living in slow motion. On a weekday afternoon there were children, teenagers, adults and the elderly all sitting outside their houses just staring, as if waiting for something.

Although there were plenty of white people in Pohnpei, the locals seemed fascinated by us and would stare for long enough to upset our English sense of decency. 'It's nothing personal,' Charles assured us. 'Micronesians stare at everyone. It's not rude here. You've probably noticed that they nod at you, and it's seen as discourteous if you don't nod back. It can be a little exhausting.'

Around every corner was a stunning view of the ocean glistening in the sun. We left the Jekyll and Hyde province of Nett, where tiny shacks sat shoulder-to-shoulder with the large, spacious houses of many of Pohnpei's wealthiest residents, and carried on around the coast. Every now and again we would see a basketball court or volleyball being played with a fishing net hoisted between two trees. Sometimes there would be athletic-looking young men playing, but mostly the improvised courts lay empty. Exercise on Pohnpei seemed to lose its appeal at a certain age.

Everyone had told us that we had to visit Nan Madol, Pohnpei's main tourist attraction – a ruined ancient city built on the ocean. Falling somewhere between Venice and Stonehenge, nobody is sure how the huge stone structures were assembled but their beauty isn't in doubt. However, Nan Madol has a sinister reputation: according to the locals, the place is sacred and houses spirits that must be respected at all costs. It's said that the first Spaniards to stumble upon the abandoned Nan Madol in the nineteenth century failed to show the necessary reverence and several members of their party died soon after in mysterious circumstances. Many Pohnpeians refuse to go anywhere near the area, so we were naturally feeling a little nervous as we approached the site. We had been driving for over an hour – certainly a lot longer than we thought would be possible on such a small island, and the quality of the roads further disintegrated as we found ourselves fighting through jungle paths in a battered Kia that had seen better days.

Finally, we came into a clearing overlooking the ocean, but a hiss from Charles told us we weren't at our destination. 'I can't believe it, I went the wrong way!' We had seen the last sign twenty minutes ago and as we disappeared further and further into the jungle I had been quietly feeling more and more sceptical that we could be headed for the biggest tourist attraction on the island. As Charles doubled back, I looked out of the window and saw with a jolt a muscled man wielding a cleaver with a severed pig's head tucked under his arm. He was approaching the car and yelling something I feared was aimed at us.

Matt had seen him too. 'Where the hell are we?' he stuttered at Charles.

'It's the slaughterhouse,' he replied as he floored the accelerator. 'Best we don't stop.'

The man with the cleaver disappeared in our rear-view mirror. He had probably been trying to offer us directions, but we were glad we hadn't waited around to find out.

When we did find Nan Madol it was worth the wait. We paid the family of the local chief $5 a head (at least five times the rate for Pohnpeians) and walked through a mangrove forest. Crabs scuttled in the mud and small birds fluttered in the brush. After five minutes we broke out of the jungle and saw the huge brick ruins rise in front of us. The main structure resembled a ship: it was an enormous but fragile-looking collection of small rocks with hundreds of smaller constructions at regular intervals separated by stretches of water. Beyond Nan Madol lay the ocean and several uninhabited islands on the horizon. The beauty of the place left us speechless. Anywhere else I had ever been, such an attraction would be crawling with tourists, but Pohnpei seemed to make no great effort to entice foreigners.

When we returned to the hotel, I felt energised but still disoriented. Since arriving I'd felt off balance thanks to jet lag and the extreme humidity, and every time I felt I was beginning to acclimatise, Pohnpei would throw something else our way. I needed to do some exercise to clear my head. Charles had mentioned a gym when he'd booked us into the hotel. When I found someone to ask downstairs, carrying my towel and bottle of water, he wordlessly beckoned for me to follow as he walked outside. We left the hotel and turned down a narrow street with small houses largely made of corrugated steel on either side. On one side of the road was an abandoned construction company premises where a host of machines lay rotting. We continued through a maze of streets with small children staring and grinning at me, and I started to wonder if gym meant, 'Can I come to your house?' in Pohnpeian.

My guide stopped at one of the houses and pointed at a path that led to some steps. When I turned to thank him, he was already walking back the way we had come. It was a gym, but about as far from Fitness First Hammersmith as it was possible to be. I entered a small room that was filled with gym equipment covered in rust. Instead of windows, there were holes in the wall which looked out on to the jungle surrounding the houses. They also let the rain through and one of the benches at the far end of the room was dripping with water. Upon hearing an odd noise coming from outside, I stuck my head out one of the holes and saw a pigpen below.

As I watched the rain pouring from the leaves of the trees outside, I tried to work out how anyone could possibly train a football team in this climate, where a sunny day can and will turn to a tropical storm with ten minutes' notice. Our first training session, rain-free and with only puddles to contend with, was clearly as good as it got. I thought again that this might be why Pohnpei has never had a decent football team. We were frustrated that we couldn't train as often as we'd like, but more than that, Matt and I were both demoralised by how difficult it was to build upon anything when we did train. Even our regulars, the players who had attended every session, seemed to hold back from us. I suspected that Ryan, the first shy boy we had met, would make a mean centre forward if only I could instil some confidence into him. Yes, he smiled and nodded and would answer questions politely, but it was obvious that he was uncomfortable, and he was desperate to leave the minute a session was over. Charles had told us that Ryan's father was the head teacher of a local school, a devoutly religious man, and I couldn't help wondering if Ryan was scared of getting in trouble for staying out too long. Most players only came for one session, or left halfway through, so there was no chance to build the enjoyable, relaxed social atmosphere that arises from playing sport with the same group of people on a regular basis: the nicknames, the in-jokes, the shared experience that so quickly becomes team spirit.

It was our job to generate enthusiasm, but the numbers were still underwhelming. I remembered with some embarrassment my brash statement on the journey to Pohnpei that I 'wouldn't know what to do if we got a hundred players every day'. I wondered whether we'd offended someone and briefly considered the possibility that Edwin Sione could be sabotaging our efforts, but then I told myself not to be so neurotic. It seemed as if the islanders we'd met were more interested in using the field as a place to meet and drink than anything we had in mind for it. Several times we had invited the gangs of men drinking there from plastic bottles to come and play, but they had dismissed us with laughter and a wave of their hand. Every now and then, usually pepped up by an early-morning dose of caffeine, Matt and I would plan training sessions we hoped to implement, but by the time we turned up to PICS Field in the evening it became clear just how far we were from being able to put our ideas into action as we waited for our suspicious gaggle of islanders to arrive. We were feeling especially dejected as, a couple of days previously, on the main road in Pohnpei, Kaselehlie Street ('kaselehlie' being an all-purpose word of greeting, like 'ciao' in Italy or 'aloha' in Hawaii), we had passed a large, slightly unsteady man whom Charles greeted warmly and beckoned us back to meet.

'This is Paul,' he said, leaving a pause for our reaction. We smiled encouragingly at him as he stood, squinting at us. When he eventually smiled back, his teeth were stained dark red from betel nut.

'Paul was Micronesia's deadliest striker in Fiji in '03. Like Gary Lineker.'

We invited him to that evening's training session. And, about an hour into it, he'd turned up, swaying and clearly a little worse for wear, then proceeded to stumble about for five minutes before leaving the pitch to vomit behind the stand.

'Gary Lineker,' said Matt as he jogged past.

Here was a player who five years ago had been one of the best Pohnpei had ever had – but like the whole game on the island, he was obviously in no shape at all now. It was clearer than ever that we needed to get far more players involved, and in a much more structured way, to have any hope of producing a successful team. It had been obvious pretty much from the outset that we couldn't trust Edwin Sione to spread the word, and that we had no choice but to do it for ourselves.

After one of the more logistically challenging workouts I've had, I found my way back from the gym and went to collect Matt en route to our appointment with Charles's television contact. As the rain lashed against the windows, we'd knocked about some mainly pun-based ideas – 'Come get a **KICK** out of soccer!', 'Get **on-side** with soccer!' and now we were due to go to the island's television HQ to see about getting a commercial broadcast. They had asked us to write up our commercial as a PowerPoint presentation, which they would put straight on air. The first of the TV station's buildings we came to was deserted with a car rusting outside it. We knocked twice but quickly retreated at the barks of a very vicious-sounding dog, clearly not happy at being woken up. We had more luck at the second building where a vast, sleepy man was joylessly punching the keyboard of a dated computer.

'Soccer?' he asked as we explained the contents of our flash drive.

'Yes.'

'OK.'

We had passed the less than vigorous screening process. It was only when we actually watched the local television stations that we understood. That night, Pohnpei's two prime-time shows were as follows:

Public Service Announcement: Soccer Soccer Soccer (15 seconds)

followed by

Land Parcel Auction Announcement (23 seconds)

We were offering free football training and they were offering discounted hectares of fertile terrain. We would have to see who the audience responded to.

Later that afternoon we had yet another meeting, this time with Churchill Edward, Pohnpei's lieutenant governor and one of the most powerful men on the island. It had taken us a week to get an appointment, but we struggled to believe Churchill had been booked up since we arrived. So far, we hadn't really seen anyone doing anything particularly hurriedly on the entire island. On the way, we decided to hand out some of our fliers. Outside the governor's office was a building site, which Charles explained was for a new municipal headquarters.

'It's paid for by the Chinese government,' he said, weaving through the piles of rubble.

It was unlike anything we had seen in Pohnpei so far. It was the tallest building on the island, a veritable skyscraper for Kolonia, incongruous with its surroundings and terribly ugly.

'People are very excited,' said Charles. 'It will have the island's first elevator.'

Charles recognised one of the builders, a former student called John, young, lean, athletic and wiry. Perfect left-back material. We gave him a flier and told him about the nightly practice. As he was writing down his phone number a Chinese man in a helmet leaped from the shadows and began to shout at us. He was clearly furious and screeched something at our would-be left back, who scuttled back to work in fear. The Chinese foreman seemed to think we were trying to unionise his worker and literally chased us off the site. As we hurried away, raindrops peppering our backs, we saw John forlornly wave at us from a distance. We never did see him at football training, and we all hoped dearly that we hadn't just cost him his job.

Charles told us that the municipal building was not the first 'friendship gesture' to be presented by the Chinese to the largely nonplussed Pohnpeians. The most impressive sporting facility in Pohnpei, the gymnasium at the College of Micronesia, was also a gift from Beijing. Our gentle colonialism had just been emphatically trumped, although the Pohnpeians appeared to have an uneasy relationship with the Chinese. While locals showed a lot of respect for the Americans and the Japanese (possibly because many families on Pohnpei had Japanese relatives, dating back to the Second World War when Japan administered the islands), their attitude to the Chinese was hostile, almost to the point of racist. Many Chinese and Vietnamese immigrants are employed to do Pohnpei's hardest jobs for tiny wages and are regarded as lackeys.

Governor Churchill Edward was tall for a Pohnpeian, with an air of authority that manifested itself in his firm handshake and unusually businesslike manner. However, unlike most of the international political leaders we were used to seeing on TV, he was wearing a Hawaiian shirt and jeans. We could see why a new HQ was necessary; his homely wooden office felt like a really well-built, cosy tree house as we sat down to explain our plans. Charles's distinguished reputation as an educator on the island – and his personal friendship with Churchill – ensured the meeting was a pleasant one and as it drew to a close we felt satisfied we had accomplished our modest goal of not offending anyone. Churchill gave us a green light to pursue our radical plan to get some people on the island together for a regular kickabout. Better than that, he even confessed his love of the game, and told us that he often walked down by the pitch and was always sure to watch any matches that took place there. The meeting was a formality, but an important sign of respect. We were quickly learning that in such a small community, it's crucial for those in office to feel they have been consulted before even the smallest project begins. To fail to do so would not only be a breach of etiquette but might well rule out the possibility of any future aid from that quarter. We decided to make a gift of one of the training shirts we had brought with us. As we proudly handed it to him, we watched him read the shirt. 'Yeovil Town.' He smiled politely and put it on his desk. If only he knew how much effort it had taken to get that shirt.

The following day's training session showed our PR efforts had been only a qualified success. It shouldn't have been difficult to reach the public, given the lack of media options available to them: any local lucky enough to have a TV would be unlikely to have cable and so had little choice but to watch our PowerPoint masterpiece. The same went for written media. We had placed a notice in the bi-weekly *Kaselehlie Press*, the only newspaper available on the island, which rounded up the limited news in the region. The front-page headline during our stay was the attention grabbing: 'FSM's Largest Solar PV Power Plant Operational in Yap', but everyone was still talking about the previous issue's revelation that an elderly man thought he had seen a crocodile in a river; an outlandish claim, given that Pohnpei's crocodile population is on a level with that of Leamington Spa's. Nonetheless, the *Kaselehlie Press* was the only source of news for the vast majority of islanders and very little of the paper was concerned with international events. The world outside Micronesia hardly seemed to exist. Indeed, when the 9/11 attacks took place many islanders didn't hear about it for over a week. I got the feeling that a full-scale Third World War could begin and only the expats would be aware of it.

We had come to Pohnpei in search of a culture where football could exist free of the ugly trappings of the media, fame and fortune, but ironically that was proving to be a great hindrance to our efforts. In a society where nobody considers football to be a way to get rich, travel the world or lure women, we could only appeal to those who genuinely had an interest in the game, but without being able to watch it on TV or read about it in the newspaper, the locals had no reason to want to play. Despite our publicity drive, the number of potential players showing up to PICS Field remained around the twenty mark. It was enough for a respectable informal game but far from the turnout we needed to suggest we could build a future for football in Pohnpei.

In England there are 40,000 association football clubs 140-odd years after football was first codified. There are 140 individual leagues comprising more than 480 divisions. One recent study suggested that 10 per cent of the population of the United Kingdom play football. We had estimated that an organised league competition on Pohnpei would require between fifty and a hundred committed players, but given the general standard of timekeeping on the island we decided we'd probably need a decent supply of willing reserves in addition. We had been so sure that giving Pohnpeians the chance to turn up, borrow all the kit they needed and see if they liked the game without any commitment on their part would yield its own results. Charles was doing his best to help us and everyone we spoke to seemed positive and willing to help, but the bottom line was that not enough people were attending. We had put football on a plate, but the majority of people weren't really interested. The twentieth and final day of our reconnaissance mission came and went with the jury still out on whether we could really bring football to Pohnpei.

On the flight back to the UK, Matt and I were in a contemplative mood. On the way out, in addition to our gaming exploits, overdosing on coffee and adrenaline, we had entertained ourselves by shouting 'Guam' at each other and discussing which country's name sounded most like a fruit. We had been ridiculously excited the first time an airline official didn't ask us to repeat 'Pohnpei' when they asked where we were going. Even a plane resembling a school technology project, a nerve-jangling landing in Chuuk en route and a barely edible sandwich hadn't dampened our enthusiasm on the Guam–Pohnpei leg.

But on the way back, we ate our tiny bags of pretzels in silence.

Charles couldn't believe his luck but even he was subdued, possibly wondering when he would next see Pohnpei, having built a whole new life in London. We were processing everything we had seen. I considered life on the island: some people walking for three miles to play football because that's the only thing they want to do. I thought of the long rows of tins of Spam in one shop that Matt and I had joked about, only for Charles to tell us that for many people on the island it was a luxury. The groups of islanders drinking by the side of the field at night, teeth stained red from betel nut.

And I couldn't stop thinking of Ryan, who had politely explained the toads' prior claim to the PICS Field, and who had been scared of the other players and sometimes the ball. And Bob and Robert, playing out sibling rivalries with two-footed tackles. I thought about Rocky, who was disappointed every time the training session was over and trudged off into the darkness. Football on the island was completely different from anything I had ever seen in the UK. And yet, at the heart of it was something I recognised. It was the feeling I remembered from the international fixtures Mark and I played in the back garden as children. It was twenty-two, or twenty or twenty-five people running after a ball for no other reason than the sheer joy of it.

As I fell asleep on the plane, I felt a little odd for a moment, and then realised I was beginning to feel dry.

3

A MARGINAL DECISION

Two weeks after returning to the UK, I was sitting with Matt in a café in Hammersmith and a rare awkward silence had descended. Our scouting mission to Pohnpei had left us with an awful lot to think about. Things had almost gone too well. Although neither of us had been willing to say so, we had both assumed before our trip that it was highly unlikely we would actually be able to coach on the island. Now we knew the role of international football coach was there for the taking, but did we really want it?

As soon as the initial euphoria faded, the deeper questions began to gather like oppressive clouds over our heads, demanding to be answered. It was one thing to spend three weeks on a tiny Pacific island, but could we actually live there? And if we could deal with the isolation, the cabin fever and the rain, how would we be able to fund ourselves, never mind the team? However much we loved football, surely we couldn't risk thousands of pounds of debt to be in charge of a daily chaotic kickaround contested by twenty islanders in various stages of intoxication. We needed the resources to set up a league – we knew from personal experience that the element of competition, of winning, would galvanise players into taking the game far more seriously.

'What we need is a sponsor,' I muttered, shivering as the door to the café swung open, momentarily exposing us to the chilly British summer.

'If a company is willing to pay thousands to put their name on a Bristol City shirt then surely there's hope,' Matt said, ignoring my glare. 'The problem might be that most English businesses are happy to do without the Micronesian market.'

We had struggled hard enough to get shirts from football clubs to take out for our first trip. We were under no illusions: it would be very tough to persuade anyone to give us money.

That night, I was discussing our problem with Lizzie over dinner. 'It's not about selling stuff in Micronesia,' she said. 'It's about offering someone the chance to buy into the story of you and Matt trying to revitalise football on Pohnpei. It's a great story, it's just that nobody knows about it.'

I chewed carefully. 'Of course, but how do we let people know? All we had to do in Micronesia to get on TV was whip up a PowerPoint presentation, avoid a dangerous-looking dog and knock on the right door. It's not quite that easy here.'

'You know how to write – and how the media works,' she said. 'Make it into an "And Finally ..." story.'

The next day, using all my journalistic savvy from my time at *Football Italia*, I pulled together a press release combining as many sound bites, simplifications and half-truths as possible. In twenty-five minutes I had created something I was relatively proud of; ideal material for filling that pesky half-inch on the left of page thirty in a daily newspaper. Once the basic story was written I made sure I angled it towards each publication I sent it to, emphasising my Bristol roots when contacting the West Country media or the fact we lived in West London for publications based in the capital. Keen not to seem like a fantasist, I borrowed Lizzie's email address to send the messages, bestowing upon her the honorary title of 'Pohnpei Soccer Press Officer'.

To: news@standard.co.uk

Subject: Londoners become football's youngest international coaches

West London residents Paul Watson and Matthew Conrad have become the youngest international coaching team in football history by taking over the national side of remote Micronesian island Pohnpei.

Conrad and Watson were appointed last week after travelling across the globe to meet Micronesian officials and at the age of 25 both are two years younger than previous youngest coach Paul Crosbie, who was appointed by the Turks & Caicos Islands at 27.

The world's third wettest climate and a staggering rate of obesity have hampered Pohnpei's previous efforts to climb football's ladder with previous results including a 16–1 drubbing against Guam, but Conrad believes they can turn Pohnpei's fortunes around.

'I've seen a lot of raw talent and with some hard work this team can surprise a few people,' the young coach insisted. 'The aim is to gain FIFA status and compete in World Cup qualification for 2014, it may be a few more years before we lift the Cup though …'

We didn't have to play the waiting game for long. Within minutes Lizzie forwarded an email from the *Fulham & Hammersmith Chronicle* asking for more details. The paper's sports specialist, a lovely chatty Northerner called Paul, told me it was the most interesting email he had received in his twenty years in the job. Our full-page article in the *Chronicle* was to prompt an avalanche of coverage. Within twenty-four hours we had appeared in the *Daily Mail*, the *Sun* and the *Daily Telegraph*. We had even been featured in magazines and newspapers across the globe. A Google search for 'Pohnpei football' turned up articles in Russia, Greece, Spain, Portugal, Romania, America and even Australia. However, the story had taken a bit of a tabloid turn and by the time it reached the biggest newspapers in the country it had acquired quite a different emphasis. I shuddered as I read the new angle in the *Sun* on 14 August 2009:

Brits to Coach 'Worst Ever Side'

BRIT Paul Watson has taken charge of the world's worst football team – on a remote island in the Pacific Ocean.

Bristol City fan Paul, 25, has become coach of tiny Pohnpei in Micronesia who have NEVER won a match.

The island, which has only 34,000 inhabitants, has a high obesity rate, the third wettest climate in the world and players often turn up late for training.

But Paul, who played football to a decent amateur standard, is confident of turning things round.

Paul took on the job with pal Matthew Conrad, 25, who will be his assistant, after bumping into a Pohnpei official in London.

Between them the pair make up the youngest national coaching team in world football.

The same sentence on Wikipedia that had attracted us to Pohnpei in the first place had come back to haunt us. 'They have never registered a win, and are said to be the weakest football team in the world.' We had only spoken to two newspapers in addition to our press release, but all kinds of desperately patronising quotes were being attributed to us: '"We were looking for a team of real no-hopers, a real footballing nonentity," Paul said. "It's fair to say Pohnpei are not very good at the moment." ''"Play Up Pohnpei' is bound to be a hit if we get any fans," Matthew grinned.'* We had certainly achieved our goal of generating publicity, but we had also inadvertently turned Pohnpei into a laughing stock.

I was mortified, but Matt tried hard to keep it in perspective.

'Dude, it's not ideal, but realistically there's no way this is going to make the *Kaselehlie Press*, especially if that crocodile's still on the loose.'

That evening we received an invitation via email to take part in the next day's BBC breakfast programme, which I seized upon as a shot at redemption. As terrifying as the words 'live TV' were, this was a great chance to set the record straight. The producer had even agreed to invite Charles, who was surprised but characteristically unfazed by being asked to appear on the nation's leading TV channel. 'I always knew I'd be famous,' he said. 'What time will I need to be up?'

The clue was in the title, but it came as something of a shock to discover exactly how early the BBC think people eat their breakfast. Sitting in a cupboard-turned-green-room and holding on to a paper cup of tea for dear life, the world of TV didn't seem so glamorous at 6.30 a.m. While Matt and I were visibly losing confidence with each passing minute as we waited for our call, Charles looked perfectly at home. Immaculately turned out, the

---

*'Play Up Pompey' or the Pompey Chimes is a chant sung by fans of Portsmouth FC at home games.

former Pohnpei FA chief didn't look worried and calmly tried to make conversation. The reason for his nonchalance was revealed as we squinted at the grim fare unfolding on the screen in front of us. 'I used to be a newsreader back in Uganda,' he said. 'Did I never mention that?' He certainly hadn't. I exchanged a look of relief with Matt; Charles would steady the ship if we got into trouble. At 6.47 a.m. we got our fifteen minutes of fame. Or, to be more precise, seven minutes. We were hurried into the tiny studio while a recorded item was playing and shook hands with the anchor whose enthusiasm for cutesy human interest stories had clearly eroded after a decade of unreasonably early mornings. 'How do you say this: Pompeii?' he asked, wearily scanning the highlighted words on a printed sheet in front of him. 'It's Pohnpei,' Matt offered. Desperate for some chat to ease the tension, I turned to Small Talk 1.01. 'Do you like football?' I ventured. 'No, not really,' he responded with a sigh. Niceties over, we sat in silence as a report on an earthquake in Sumatra came to its conclusion.

The interview went by in a blur. Charles handled the first few questions, which mostly focused on establishing why we were remotely newsworthy. I had drunk a gallon of tea and failed to sleep the night before, so my dual objectives were to avoid either falling off the stool or wetting myself. I succeeded in both and even managed to transmit reasonably eloquently my passion for football and my desire to make an impact in Pohnpei. It came as a relief but also a disappointment that we weren't asked about the 'worst team in the world' tag and so didn't have a chance to counter it. The phones didn't exactly ring off the hook following our early-morning appearance, probably because nobody in their right mind is watching TV before 7 a.m. Not even our parents had watched live.

Meanwhile, the quest for sponsorship was going badly. It was horribly reminiscent of the barrage of emails we'd sent asking for shirts before our first trip. It was hard to see why any sane person would say yes. Rather than sit around and wait for a backer to step forward, we began to contact companies with possible business interests in Micronesia. Unsurprisingly, emails to the Bank of Hawaii, Bank of Guam and Toyota from a Hotmail address begging sponsorship for a minority sport on a fictional-sounding Pacific island were met with a wall of silence. The big hope was always going to be Continental Airlines. American giants Continental are a dominant force in the Micronesian economy. They are the only airline that flies to the region, running an island-hopper service that scoops up passengers from almost all the islands between Guam and Hawaii. Given the distances between the Micronesian islands, the only travel option for someone who doesn't want to spend a few weeks on a boat is to fly Continental, and having such a monopoly allows you to name whatever price you want. A one-and-a-half-hour flight from Pohnpei to Guam can cost as much as £1,000, and even with special residents' rates it is usually around £600 – a fortune in a nation where the average annual salary is just £6,000.

We hadn't exactly received value for money on our first trip on Continental Micronesia. However, we had learned that Micronesians by nature aren't inclined to complain, and Continental know it. In a bid to land Continental as sponsors we adopted a strategy of bugging them endlessly by all means possible. It was a strategy born partly of increasing desperation and partly of wishful thinking that a global giant would see £20,000 as a small price to pay to shut us up. The good news was that after just thirty-five emails, twenty-four answerphone messages and letters to Continental offices in Houston, New York and Cleveland we had an answer. The bad news was that the answer read:

> Thank you for your email to Continental Airlines. We regret to inform that we cannot oblige as Continental already sponsors Guam's rugby team. We would see this as a conflict of interests.

They had spoken. Their sponsorship of a team playing a different sport in a different country would prevent them considering our request. We had failed in our bid to get sponsorship. However hard we tried to fight it, there was a creeping realisation that we would need the help of FIFA.

Our promise: For the game, for the world. Our mission: Develop the game, touch the world, build a better future. So crows the website of football's governing body, but any football fan knows better. For all its grandiose claims, FIFA is little more than the butt of jokes for lovers of the beautiful game. To us, the organisation seems to spend most of its time cooking up ways to look after the richest members and the rest trying to find a new baffling clause for the offside rule every year. At heart, like so many other big multinational organisations, FIFA is a collection of rich men who have no intention of rocking the boat and altering the structure that allowed them to get rich in the first place. In a world of long-standing alliances and multimillion-pound business interests, what hope did a couple of twenty-something British lads have of being taken seriously?

Things were made even more difficult by the fact that we were only representing Pohnpei, just one of four Micronesian islands.

We hadn't allowed ourselves to think about it yet, but in order to be recognised as a nation, we knew we would have to take Yap, Chuuk and Kosrae under our umbrella regardless of the vast geographical distance between the islands. The general consensus in Pohnpei was that football hadn't been played on the other three islands for some time, but even so, to try and pass ourselves off as representing the whole of Micronesia would cause outrage there.

Previous efforts to unite the FSM under one banner for football had failed, largely due to the costs involved in flying players between the islands to train together. With airfares sky high, the last Micronesia team of the late 1990s and early 2000s had to be based on Yap with a couple of token Pohnpeians invited as a political gesture. The Yapese bias had caused resentment in Pohnpei, the Chuukese had been livid that Pohnpeians had been invited at all, while the whole thing made little impression on the sleepy island of Kosrae. The task of creating lasting national sporting structures in countries as distant as England and Hungary had always proven difficult, while FIFA had always proved uncompromising and refused to consider funding requests until every island was represented in one squad. But without any funding or incentive to create a unified team, there was no way of showing them what they needed to see. It was a Catch-22 situation.

But there was one other possibility. Maybe we didn't need FIFA after all. Right at the beginning of our research an organisation called the Nouvelle Fédération-Board had cropped up. Founded by a couple of football-mad Belgians, the NF-Board was established as an association for those states not recognised by FIFA. The rules are somewhat more relaxed than FIFA's: if you can muster a team, a kit and a sense of regional identity then you are in. The list of members is a who's who of geographical anomalies, political and religious taboos and delusions of grandeur. At its most noble, the NF-Board represents Tibet and Greenland, states that otherwise have been left out in the cold by football's authorities. On the other end of the scale, Sealand, a former Second World War sea fort in the North Sea without a blade of grass or a goal net to its name, has been granted ingress.

The NF-Board also has its version of FIFA's World Cup. The VIVA World Cup was played in Lapland under the midnight sun in 2008 and pitted Iraqi Kurdistan against a team representing the local Sápmi people in its opening game. The five-team tournament ended with an emphatic victory for Padania, a team representing an Italian political party called the Lega Nord, which believes the north of Italy should be an independent nation. Their side boasted several players who had seen the bright lights of Serie A. The next VIVA World Cup had been awarded to Gozo in Malta and I suspected Pohnpei would be welcomed with open arms by the NF-Board. Could our search for international funding and recognition result in taking a team of shell-shocked Pacific Islanders to Malta? Energised, I tracked down a book called *Outcasts: The Lands that FIFA Forgot* and read the history of non-FIFA football from cover to cover. With a thousand questions forming in my head, I decided to track down the author Steve Menary and after a few days I got an email saying he'd be free in London later that afternoon.

I phoned Matt to tell him the news.

'Great,' was all he said. His voice flat.

'Well, don't go too crazy.'

'I got in,' he mumbled.

'What?'

'USC. I've been offered a place. I'm in.'

I had more or less forgotten that Matt had applied for a film course at the University of Southern California. He had never mentioned it without the caveat that he 'would never get in'. But he had. It was a bittersweet moment. I was honestly delighted for Matt – you couldn't be his friend and not know what this meant to him – but from a selfish point of view things had taken a demoralising twist.

'It would mean I'd have to go to LA for ten months. I wouldn't be able to come back to Pohnpei.'

'Mate, you've got to say yes.'

'But it feels as if we could really do something on Pohnpei.'

I began to think of all the challenges involved in developing football in Pohnpei and couldn't imagine doing them alone. We agreed to talk properly later and I went to meet Steve Menary feeling slightly dazed. In a dingy old pub just off Tottenham Court Road we settled down to discuss Pohnpei's footballing future. In his time as a journalist, Steve has passionately fought the corner of football's most desperate causes. Within minutes of meeting him we were discussing the state of the game on the islands of Wallis & Futuna. Not your average pub football chat.

'I can't get any answer when I call the Wallis & Futuna FA number now,' Steve said sadly. 'I think they've probably gone the same way as Nauru.'

Nauru, officially the world's most obese country, is a tiny island a couple of thousand miles east of Pohnpei. On an outpost so isolated that planes land on the main road, there aren't an awful lot of leisure activities. During the 1970s Nauru became one of the world's richest countries per head of population due to its phosphate mines, which provided a valuable resource Australia couldn't get enough of. FIFA briefly started to support football there and things looked bright. But the phosphate mines were over-exploited, the government invested its money badly and when the country inevitably went bankrupt, FIFA withdrew its funding. Australian Rules Football still has a hold, but soccer is dead. Wallis & Futuna, like several other countries in the Pacific, had fallen victim to the FIFA Catch 22 – they had been suspended for a lack of activity and thus become ineligible for the funding they needed to kick-start the game.

'FIFA would never consider funding a Pohnpei team,' Steve said, confirming our fears. 'They wouldn't take you seriously because you don't represent the whole of Micronesia.'

'How about the NF-Board – would they have us?' I asked.

'They'd take you in an instant, there's no doubt about that. The problem is that they can't provide any funding at all. The teams who turn up to tournaments like the VIVA World Cup have to find the cash on their own. It's a miracle that any of them manage it. In the build-up to each competition, the number of competitors always drops rapidly and it's pot luck as to who actually turns up.'

Steve told me that for all its noble intentions, structurally the NF-Board was not much more than a group of Belgian friends who shared an infatuation with football. Unlike FIFA's World Cup, companies were reluctant to sponsor the VIVA equivalent. Putting your name to a tournament pitting disputed territories such as Tibet and West Papua against each other, for a title which might be contested by eight, five or just two other teams, doesn't represent the soundest of investments.

'From your point of view, the biggest problem with Pohnpei joining the NF-Board is that it could piss FIFA off,' Steve explained. 'It could be seen as an act of rebellion and FIFA representatives certainly know how to hold a grudge. You run the risk of setting Micronesia back in the long term.'

With Steve's warning ringing in my ears, I went home and tore up the NF-Board application forms. For the first time I felt a sobering sense of responsibility. To indulge my own personal fantasy, I could endanger the development of the game in Micronesia for a generation. It just wasn't worth the risk.

Later that night over a few drinks, Matt and I talked about what could be done. He had formally accepted the USC place, and although he wasn't going to be in Pohnpei with me in person, he was determined to help in any way he could.

'It might even work out really well,' he said. 'Like a pincer movement on either side of the Pacific.'

We had been home for six weeks and still nobody seemed interested in stepping forward as a sponsor. Added to this, the only chance of getting an international match and any funding was by uniting the Federated States of Micronesia – a task that posed a myriad political and logistical issues. I wondered if maybe it was time to cut my losses and write off the first Pohnpei trip as an expensive holiday. I had never been the kind of person who did things on my own. I can't even eat in a restaurant alone without feeling intensely awkward. The thought of returning to Pohnpei without Matt and trying to build a life there was incredibly daunting. I wouldn't even have Charles Musana to watch over me as he had on our first trip. Yet I had already committed to Pohnpei in so many ways. I had quit my job, given up my flat, and Lizzie and I had geared ourselves up for a long-distance relationship. It also occurred to me that if I never returned to Pohnpei I would be a fraud. The newspaper articles, the TV appearance, the radio interviews would all seem like a student prank and one that had raised false hopes.

It was mid-August. A decision had to be made by the start of September: that was the deadline I'd set to ensure I didn't continue moping and losing money indefinitely. I was already starting to borrow from friends and family to get by and I wasn't even doing anything to show for it. I was still perched agonisingly on the fence when an email arrived that decisively tipped things in Pohnpei's favour. Charles had made reference to a talented young player called Dilshan when we visited Pohnpei, but he had been away visiting his brother in Manila during our stay and I had thought nothing more of him. However, an email from Dilshan, a Sri Lankan native who had lived on Pohnpei for nine years, lifted the gloom that had gathered.

From: Dilshan Senarathgoda
Subject: Pohnpei Soccer

Hi Paul,

I'm devastated that I missed your visit. I hope everything went well and you got to see how much enthusiasm there is for football in Pohnpei. I know that you met my cousin Ryan – he is becoming a really good player. I've been training a team of young locals for a year and they're getting good, but you may not have met them because they didn't train while I was away. Soccer is still very much a developing sport here and we don't get many opportunities to move forward and grow but we play five nights a week. We sincerely appreciate your help and everyone here is looking forward to your return.

A Marginal Decision

The email barely contained any specific details but it was enough for me. I wouldn't be working on my own; I would be working with Dilshan, evidently an established and respected figure in the footballing community. If there was just one team of committed players we could build from there. My fears of holding endless games of three-and-in had been allayed. I had needed only the slightest reassurance to allow me to jet off to Micronesia with justifiable cause for hope. True, an email from somebody I had never met telling me a dozen people were regularly playing football of some kind wasn't much, but it was enough. I booked my ticket to return to Micronesia.

4

IN A LEAGUE OF THEIR OWN

I'd travelled halfway round the world; I felt, looked and smelt terrible; but I was in Pohnpei. As I entered the arrivals hall, Dilshan was nowhere to be seen, though this was not entirely surprising as my flight had been delayed by three days. The trip had begun with a heart-wrenching, tearful goodbye to Lizzie as she went to work and I set off for Heathrow and a series of flights that would carry me thousands of miles into the unknown. Well, semi-unknown. I'd made the first trip knowing (a) I'd be coming home in three weeks and (b) I'd have Matt for company. This time I was going on my own for at least six months to a Pacific island I barely knew, with only a handful of emails from a man I'd never met to reassure me that the whole venture would be anything but a disaster.

The journey certainly hadn't been plain sailing. In fact it might have been quicker to sail from Hammersmith Bridge. I spent the moments before take-off at Heathrow in denial that I was leaving, but the further I got from London, the more I had to convince myself that the decision had been made and I had to make the best of it. Since Matt wouldn't be there to distract, annoy and put up with me in equal measure, I had decided to bring lots and lots of books, but on the trip to Manila I couldn't concentrate on anything. For the Manila–Guam flight, I had been designated an emergency-exit seat with an embarrassment of legroom. Better still, I had a whole row to myself; I almost felt lonely, I had so much space. And then it all went wrong. Two minutes before take-off time the chirpy cabin crew told us to deplane owing to a technical fault. I winced, both at the word 'deplane' and at the idea of a technical fault. Back in the waiting room, we waited. And waited.

After five hours Continental deemed it necessary to inform us that we were delayed, but wouldn't be drawn on when we might take off. I read and read and read but was disturbed regularly by the livid Texan sitting next to me, who insisted on elbowing my ribs every five minutes in order to get my attention for his latest venomous take on Continental's incompetence. After ten hours in a waiting room and with my ribs feeling decidedly sore, we were sent to hotels. The plane couldn't be fixed. The next available flight to Pohnpei was in three days. I tried calling my hotel, Nara Gardens, to warn them that I would be delayed, only to be met with a piercing whistle that nearly ruptured my eardrum. I sent Dilshan an email asking him to pass on the message.

So I was fairly jaded when, after my four-day journey, I staggered through the 'Arrivals' door at Pohnpei International Airport to be met by nobody. I looked down at my two huge bags stuffed with football boots, a set of blue training shirts and two dozen pairs of white socks and became aware that I was sweating profusely. Part of me was relieved at the absence of a welcoming committee. I'd had visions of a gang of enraged Pohnpeians, furious at the *Sun*'s ridicule of their football team, running me off the island with machetes. A large group sat chewing in sync, waiting for someone else. Judging by their College of Micronesia T-shirts I guessed it was for an American volunteer teacher or a new student intake from Chuuk. They certainly weren't there to hail the arrival of Pohnpei's new football coach.

It struck me that I had no idea what Dilshan looked like and I mentally kicked myself for not asking him to email me a picture. I knew that he was the older cousin of Ryan, the shy keepy-uppy guy, but that was all I had to go on. Dilshan would have an easier time spotting me. I was the bright white, sweaty mess with an England shirt sticking to him and a swarm of mosquitoes hosting a celebratory feast on his leg. I noticed the smell, that distinctive damp smell of Pohnpei that I had come to love and hate during my last trip.

'Mr Watson?'

I turned expectantly and was surprised to see an elderly man in a Hawaiian shirt holding his hand out to me. I was pretty sure this wasn't Dilshan.

'I run Nara Gardens,' he said as I shook his hand. 'We heard about the flight not coming in on Sunday, so we knew you'd be on this one.

'Please,' he said, gesturing me aboard a beat-up mini-van.

The allure of a shower was so great that any thought of sticking it out and waiting for Dilshan evaporated. I had his phone number; I would call him as soon as I felt human again.

Even in my semi-conscious state I was dazzled by the blue of the water and the bright green of the forest surrounding the jagged outcrop of Sokehs Rock, Pohnpei's most notable landmark. My driver proved to be a man of few words, and I was grateful for the respite. At Nara Gardens I headed straight for the shower.

As I pulled on clean clothes I heard a knock on the door. I staggered over and pulled it open.

'Sorry I'm late,' a voice said. 'I thought Nara Gardens was the name of some chick you knew out here.' I had finally met Dilshan Senarathgoda.

My first impression was that Dilshan looked like a footballer. Had he been at the airport on time, I reckoned I would have been able to pick him out on that basis alone. Dilshan was average height for the island – a few inches shorter than me. Before he shook my hand he pushed his sunglasses up on to his forehead and I noticed he wore ear studs, which glistened below his Mohican haircut.

'I've lived in Pohnpei for nine years but I can honestly say I've never been to this place,' Dilshan explained. 'Let's go get something to eat.'

He led the way to his car, which was easily the best maintained I had seen on the island so far, and drove us to the Ocean View Hotel, where we began to lay out our plan for football in Pohnpei. I thought of the optimistic to-do list Matt and I had drawn up at his kitchen table:

1) Get sponsor.
2) Set up league.
3) Pick Pohnpei team.
4) ~~Play~~ Win international fixture.
5) Unite disparate islands as one Micronesian team, qualify for FIFA funding and usher in new age of contentment and prosperity.

So far number 1 was proving tricky but we could at least make a proper go of 2. It would also give me the best chance of scouting players for 3.

I was most interested to hear about the Island Pit Bulls, the team of local players Dilshan had been training that it seemed we somehow hadn't met during our first trip.

'They're really good guys,' Dilshan said. 'When I first met them they had no idea how to play, but they've come so far in a year. Now we always beat the Internationals.'

I'd heard about International FC before: the team of assorted non-Pohnpeians who turn up to PICS Field regularly. I'd met several of them during our earlier kickarounds. Dilshan informed me that the team usually consisted of a few Americans, a couple of Fijians, some Australians and a couple of Englishmen. I was surprised to find myself disappointed to hear that there were other Englishmen on the island; I had quite liked the idea of being the only Brit mad enough to voyage to this obscure dot on the globe.

After such a long build-up to my meeting with Dilshan I was relieved to find him so easy to talk to, but I couldn't help but wonder whether I matched up to his expectations. A mammoth sleep-debt had rotted my brain and I was melting in the heat. Dilshan, on the other hand, seemed ice cool in every way. He was completely unfazed by the temperature – though I suppose his being Sri Lankan helped with that – and spoke in a slow, deep voice with an unusual quasi-Caribbean accent. It was only after three hours and four beers that we arrived at the real business.

'We need to set up a proper league,' I said, swatting away a dragonfly the size of a dinner plate. 'If we can create some real competition, I think we would be able to get to a proper Pohnpei team.'

'We should definitely do that, man,' Dilshan agreed. 'First, though, you've got to meet the Pit Bulls. If you're going to be their coach, they need to get to know you. Don't look so worried, they're all really excited to meet you.'

I felt a rush of anxiety as it struck home that I was going to have to be a leader. The nerves didn't get a chance to foment, however, as we decided to go in search of entertainment. Being a tiny island, Pohnpei doesn't exactly have a wealth of nightlife options. In fact, it has two: the Rusty Anchor and Club Flamingo. Matt and I had sampled both on our earlier visit, though to be honest my memory of either was rather hazy. The Rusty Anchor is an American expat bar that would provide stunning views over the bay for daytime visitors. Sadly, it's only open at night, when it's populated by a handful of regulars who drink Corona or Bud Light and listen to 1970s guitar rock. Every month or so the island's only band, Wetter Than Seattle, puts on a gig and the expat community turns out in force.

Club Flamingo is more of a dancehall and is largely visited by locals who mix rum and beer and grind against each other to the beat of the cheesiest of songs, often given an 'island remix'. Although Pohnpeians are by nature very peaceful people and keen to avoid conflict, Flamingo is often closed so the owners can repair the damage from a brawl. Pohnpeians know how to handle their betel nut and sakau but not, it would seem, their alcohol.

We made for the Rusty Anchor, primarily because it is home to Kolonia's only public pool tables. Passing through an unmarked door and down a long dark corridor, we eventually emerged into a dimly lit bar. Maritime flags hung above two pool tables, and a notice board on the wall displayed pictures of a twenty-foot fish caught just off shore along with some pictures marked 'Halloween', though no clue was provided to the year in which they had been taken.

As we entered, we were still drawing up a plan of action.

'There need to be teams for the best players to play against,' I said. 'If a Pohnpei team is to get off the ground, the players we have need to get fitter and be tested.'

A grin spread across Dilshan's face.

'I think I know one team, for a start, and I think I can just about arrange a meeting with their captain.'

Dilshan nodded to the barman, and to three other punters, and then shook hands and patted the shoulder of a tall American with an impressive moustache who was sitting at the bar.

'Paul, this is Steve Finnen,' Dilshan said. 'The captain of International FC.'

'Hardly the captain,' Steve said, laughing as he shook my hand. 'I'm not sure a team like International FC can really have a captain – we pretty much take anyone we can get.'

Within such a small community, you don't necessarily have to stick to one role; the same person can be at once the best doctor, tennis player and wine authority. A brief conversation revealed Steve to be Micronesia's most in-demand lawyer, a prominent member of the Rotary Club, the bass player in Wetter Than Seattle and the figurehead for Frisbee and rugby, as well as International FC's de facto skipper.

'If there's a league, you can guarantee an International team will be there,' Steve said. 'We should be fine for numbers if we can persuade enough of the student teachers at the Seventh Day Adventist School. Besides, why don't you play for us?'

'Oh, I don't –'

'I think you should do it,' Dilshan interrupted. 'Playing against the local guys is the best way to be seen as one of them.'

It was agreed. I would play for International FC in the Pohnpei league – a league that, for the first time, felt as though it might be beginning to take shape.

I woke up the next morning to the sound of torrential rain and dogs fighting. It didn't take me long to realise I wasn't in London. My first priority for the day was to call Lizzie. We had agreed that I would try to call at 8 a.m., which would be 10 p.m. in England. I grabbed my laptop bag and made a dash for the FSM Telecom Centre – an uphill sprint of around two hundred metres. The Telecom Centre is a small building with a vast satellite dish protruding from it. Offering twenty-four-hour internet access (and a twenty-four-hour smell of disinfectant), this place would become my link to the outside world. I bought a $20 internet card, loaded Skype and phoned Lizzie. My heart beat double time as it rang and rang and then finally connected. From over 8,000 miles away I could hear her voice as though she were in the next room. From her end, though, I might as well have been on the next planet, since she couldn't hear a word I was saying. I hung up and redialled and this time we were able to talk for three minutes before we were cut off. I repeated the process twelve times in twenty minutes before the line went dead and refused to reconnect. I took my computer to the counter to ask for help.

'Is finished,' a girl with three gold teeth and a grey shirt saying 'Keep Diabetes At Bay!' told me.

'Finished? But that was twenty dollars!'

She shrugged. The rain pelted down, drenching a shirtless man sifting through the outside bin. The security guard on the door chased him off. Having parted with another $20, I composed an email to FIFA describing our plans for a league and asking how Pohnpei could go about getting some assistance with development. I sent it to Tai Nicholas, the secretary general of the Oceania Football Confederation, within whose jurisdiction Micronesia lies. I was astonished when I received a reply almost immediately. Tai, a genial New Zealander, was in more or less the same time zone as me and seemed to be on more or less the same wavelength as well. He offered his full support. The only problem was that the OFC couldn't help, having decided some years earlier that responsibility for Micronesia should be transferred to the East Asian Football Federation, which had more money to throw around. Tai was happy to direct me to the right person at the EAFF and wished me all the best.

Dilshan was an hour late picking me up for my first meeting with the Pit Bulls, but I appreciated the chance to collect my thoughts. The weather had completely changed and it was now boiling hot, the neighbourhood dogs lay apathetically looking defeated and I felt a series of apparently invisible bugs biting my legs. Just a week earlier I had been shivering in jeans and a coat in London; now I felt overdressed in shorts and a T-shirt.

Dilshan's immaculate car pulled up and he gestured for me to get in.

'Sorry I'm late again,' he said. 'I had to take my mum up to the college.'

Dilshan lived with his parents in a flat halfway between Nara Gardens and PICS Field. The drawback in having a car was that he was constantly called into action as a taxi service. His mum, a lovely tiny Sri Lankan woman, had decided she would never drive, so every day Dilshan had to take his parents to the College of Micronesia, where they both worked, near the administrative capital of Palikir some twenty minutes away. We drove past the Olympic Committee office and the new Chinese-funded town hall, stopping entirely to allow a dog to amble across the road, and again for a car to pull off a nineteen-point turn in the middle of Kolonia's busiest street. Finally, we arrived at PICS Field. The grass was overgrown and wild and areas of the pitch had been churned up terribly. I took it as a positive: proof that someone had been playing football.

A small group of boys were on the stone steps next to the pitch, laughing while someone's phone played an Akon song. Several of them had boots on and a few were wearing the Yeovil shirts we'd brought on our first trip. As we got closer I recognised the two Welson brothers, Joseph (famed for having the hardest shot in Pohnpei) and Charles (the goalkeeper), engaged in a wrestling bout. They straightened up when I approached and I tried to catch Joseph's eye to say hello, but he walked over and sat down. I spied the distinctive long rat tail of Rocky Henly, the training addict, and opposite him Dilshan's cousin Ryan and Roger from Nett, the youngest players who had attended training. It suddenly dawned on me that any potential we had seen in August wasn't natural talent at all but actually the result of Dilshan's hard work. The other six or seven figures were strangers to me. It was hard to know what to say. Dilshan had taught these boys how to play. He had built up their trust over the course of many months. I had pretty much pitched up out of the blue and was so very … British. It all felt horribly colonial. However much I told myself that I was actually here for vaguely altruistic reasons – I had brought boots, kit, balls and I intended to teach them anything I could – I just couldn't help worrying that they would have seen the way the media had covered the story back in the UK and think I was here to cash in and laugh at their expense.

The players stared at me. Akon was silenced mid-squeak.

'Hey, guys, our new coach wants to talk to us,' Dilshan said. I felt my heart begin to race.

Everyone was now silent except for Roger, who apparently

hadn't heard Dilshan and was singing a bizarre falsetto version of a popular island song.

'Roger!' Dilshan roared.

'Yes?' He whipped round with a grin on his face.

'Shut up.'

'OK,' Roger said, still beaming.

I stutteringly outlined my idea of a league, forming a Pohnpei team from the best native players, and eventually playing a friendly against another island or nation. I had no idea what they were thinking and it crossed my mind that some of them might not even be able to understand me at all. Some of the seated figures gave me encouraging (or perhaps it was pitying) smiles, but one player, whom Dilshan addressed as Micah, glowered with hostility. After I had finished, Dilshan reiterated what I had said, still mostly in English but leaving out the jargon and adding some more islander-friendly terminology, and received a much more enthusiastic response. We sat for a while as the players spoke animatedly amongst themselves, almost entirely in Pohnpeian. I was getting a crash course in the local language, and the first thing I noticed was that all the players addressed each other as 'nahn', equating to the English 'mate'. The focus of attention was Charles Welson, who was attempting to chat up six young Pohnpeian girls sitting fifty metres away. I had no idea what he was saying, but the language of bad chat-up lines is pretty much universal. Charles gamely shrugged off a laughing rejection from one girl and moved on to the next. Each time he finished speaking the rest of the players would hoot with laughter.

'The amazing thing is that sometimes he gets one to go home with him!' Dilshan whispered, as if we were watching a nature documentary. 'Rocky's just as bad when he's drunk. He's technically got a girlfriend but he always says he should be allowed to have four or five.'

Dilshan told me that he had a long-term girlfriend. The only problem was that she lived 700 kilometres away in the neighbouring island of Chuuk, where Dilshan had stayed for several years before coming to Pohnpei, and they could only see each other every couple of months or so. While his Pit Bulls teammates chased any female they saw, Dilshan drove them wild by fending off the advances of the same girls Charles and Rocky had spent hours hollering at. Dilshan wasn't interested in cheating, but there were pragmatic reasons as well as emotional ones for his faithfulness.

'My girlfriend has cousins everywhere on Pohnpei, man,' he laughed. 'If I did anything she'd find out in minutes and one of her cousins would probably cut my dick off!'

Eventually, we left. 'That went really well, man; they like you,' Dilshan said as we drove off.

How could he possibly know that? I wondered.

The night before, my concern had been that, after the Pit Bulls and the Internationals, we would run out of teams. Two teams don't make a league anywhere except in Scotland. And Spain. But in any case Dilshan reminded me that there had been a generation of footballers before this one: Charles Musana's contemporaries. Charles had told us about them, the Local Warriors, and they would all still be in their thirties or forties with years of play left in them. So that evening, after my speech at PICS, Dilshan drove us to meet the captain of the Warriors, the governor's cousin John (pronounced June) Ehsa. John was a powerful man on the island with extensive business interests and a fearsome reputation.

Turning off Kolonia's main street, we went past the Spanish Wall – one of a few remaining vestiges of Spanish colonial rule – and down a series of increasingly narrow and bumpy roads. Eventually we hit a cul-de-sac and the car headlights revealed a group of burly men under a tin roof drinking sakau. One of the men approached the car, squinting like a vampire caught in sunlight, and judging by his paunch I guessed he probably wasn't a footballer. It felt a little like a mafia rendezvous.

'We're here to see John,' explained Dilshan, who was still wearing his sunglasses. 'It's about football.'

Satisfied, the paunchy man moved back into the shadows and was soon replaced by an equally paunchy though well-muscled islander. This was John.

'How is the football?' he asked Dilshan. 'I seen you guys up at PICS a few times, you look good.'

'We want to set up a league for Pohnpei. This is Paul. He's from England and is coaching our local guys to make them good,' Dilshan said. 'We were hoping the Local Warriors might play.'

'I think they will play,' John said. 'If there is a competition they will want to play.'

John moved towards me and stopped far too close to me for comfort. Suddenly he thrust out his hand and grabbed mine.

'Thank you for coming here,' he growled. 'Anything you ever need is yours. I love football. Anything you like.'

And the meeting was over. We thanked John and beat our retreat.

'It's great they'll be in the league,' I said as we slowly retraced our steps.

'The Local Warriors won't be in the league,' Dilshan laughed.

'But John just said ...'

'He was just saving face,' Dilshan explained patiently. 'He couldn't be seen to say no. What he means is that he won't stand in our way if we have a league. It's really good we consulted him.'

I realised how much I had to learn about island ways. The dialogue of the meeting I had witnessed with John was very different in translation. Dilshan was my only hope of understanding what people truly meant.

The following evening we returned to PICS Field for the weekly kickaround Dilshan organised. I was intrigued to see who would come out of the woodwork. Rocky was already there, jogging around the running track – I wondered if he ever went home. The twins Robert and Bob Paul were early arrivals and I noticed that Robert had one of the Yeovil shirts on, while Bob was wearing a plain black top. As I watched the two identical men saunter towards the field, Ryan shuffled up to me wearing a shiny new Real Madrid shirt and equally shiny Nike boots.

'Bob and Robert used to play with the Local Warriors but they got sick of the older guys not turning up, so they left,' he whispered. 'Robert said he was joining Dilshan's Pit Bulls, so Bob decided he would make his own team.'

Ryan also told me that Robert had represented his country before but didn't have fond memories of it. He was part of the Micronesia team that travelled to the South Pacific Games in Fiji in 2003, but he had been a substitute for the entire event, not even setting foot on the pitch. Before I could ask Ryan more, the sudden blaring of loud hip-hop made us turn, to see that a remarkably well-maintained truck had arrived being driven by someone I vaguely recognised. A grinning, overweight Micronesian slammed the door shut and bellowed a greeting to Dilshan, who was nearly a hundred yards away. Everyone seemed to know him and everyone was pleased to see him.

'You remember me. I'm Alika,' he said, and, with overpowering enthusiasm hugged us both.

I realised that I had met him during a drunken evening in Club Flamingo on my first trip. He'd sat with us, telling us at great length that he used to be a goalkeeper, but then after that we hadn't seen much of Alika, who had been too busy dancing with a string of different women and sinking a vast quantity of beer. But now he was here and, better still, he had goalkeeping gloves.

'I told you I was a goalkeeper,' he said to me, waving the gloves in my face with pride. 'And if I could get rid of this, I'd be the best on the island,' he added, rubbing his protruding belly.

A car pulled up and Steve Finnen got out wearing a red England away kit. As we stood there, trying to work out how soon it would rain, we were joined by another couple of members of International FC.

'Paul, this is Simon Ellis; he's from England, too.'

I nodded at him, again slightly miffed at having my illusions of intrepid exploration punctured. To make it worse, it turned out he was originally from Bath, just a few miles down the road from where I'd grown up.

'And this is Damian. They both work on a marine conservation project.'

We all spoke for a while and my childish hostility dwindled. They were extremely friendly and very enthusiastic about the idea of a league – and about having a new player for International FC. While I was talking to the expats, almost all the Pit Bulls had arrived. I could see Rocky, Roger and Joseph aimlessly juggling a ball in a muddy puddle on the edge of the box while Alika bounced up and down in the goalmouth calling for them to hit shots at him. Meanwhile Dilshan had inflated one of the new balls I'd brought over and was hitting a string of inch-perfect free kicks in the other goalmouth.

With light rain starting to fall we quickly divided into two teams and began a game. Charles and Joseph Welson pitched up and were gently mocked by Dilshan for being late, despite living a matter of metres from PICS. Out of habit, I glanced around nervously, looking for Edwin Sione. The 'chicken man' had been conspicuously absent since my first trip with Matt, and I'd heard rumours circulating that he wasn't happy with the direction Pohnpeian football was taking. Another less than friendly face had arrived in the form of Micah – the Pit Bull who had seemed hostile at my introductory meeting. I was surprised to see that Micah was really very good. He flew up and down the wing and naturally had a good eye for a pass. He was perfect winger material.

The flow of the game was very different from the chaos of the previous summer. Dilshan, who was on the opposing team to me, controlled the pace, effortlessly firing through balls and telling each player where and when to run. His control naturally set him apart from the other players on the pitch and you could see that they relied on him for every movement. I threw myself into marking Dilshan and it became an entertaining battle. As I struggled in the heat I was surprised and impressed to see Simon and Damian covering huge distances without any sign of strain. The less mobile Steve, who had a long-standing knee problem, threw himself into the physical side and full-blooded challenges rained in. Roger was baffling me. The seventeen-year-old seemed to have boundless energy but no idea how to direct it. He would run seventy-five yards to make a tackle only to dribble the ball sideways then backwards before blasting it off the pitch altogether. While other players cursed and yelled, Roger smiled constantly and broke into song at regular intervals. I turned to Ryan for some background on Roger as I knew the two were the same age and went to school together.

'Is Roger drunk?' I asked.

'No way. He's substance free, like me. Roger doesn't smoke, drink or chew,' Ryan asserted. 'He's just the happiest person I know.'

Here were two seventeen-year-olds on a football pitch and neither of them would touch a drop of alcohol. I felt a long way from home.

Dilshan scored first with a curling free kick after he had been poleaxed by a late arrival: Dilshan's uncle and Ryan's dad Johnson. We fought back, but our forward Bob wasted several good chances by taking far too many touches, much to the annoyance of his strike partner Joseph. It was obvious that the two couldn't stand each other. Bob was also antagonising his brother Robert, who, as usual, was on the other team playing in defence. Bob was faster and repeatedly beat Robert to the ball, taunting him in front of the other players. But more often than not Robert would have the last laugh as Bob dribbled aimlessly and could easily be dispossessed. When the ball eventually found its way to Joseph it became apparent why he had been so frustrated at Bob's selfish tactics. The teenager received the ball on the edge of the box, took one touch and blasted it past his brother Charles in the opposing goal. One-all. He grinned briefly, showing a glint of gold teeth and red gums, and then stared at the ground, shaking off any attempt to congratulate him.

Dilshan seemed certain to score again minutes later after Micah trotted down the wing and cut back an inviting ball to him, but Alika produced a magnificent diving save to deny him. On the rebound, Dilshan blasted a piledriver from five yards out but Alika fearlessly flung himself in the way, taking its full force in his stomach. The blow would have been enough to leave most people winded and writhing on the floor, but Alika merely chuckled and playfully slapped Dilshan on the behind.

'You've got to do better than that,' he said.

I was staggered. Alika had clearly played before. It wasn't just his astonishing athleticism that marked him out (in spite of his paunch), it was also his communication skills. While the rest of the players seemed scared to shout at each other, even to ask for the ball, Alika maintained a constant, confident dialogue with his defenders.

At 1–1 the game finished, as with all games in Pohnpei, when it became pitch black. Fighting back my trepidation, my first port of call was Micah.

'I'm really impressed,' I said. 'You played very well.'

For a second Micah met my eye, but he thought better of it and walked off without a word. Everyone retreated to the side of the pitch to take off their boots and I was formally introduced to Johnson, who was the head teacher of the Seventh Day Adventist School and incredibly friendly. It was hard to believe that the man who upended Dilshan so many times on the pitch could be so mild-mannered and courteous.

'Johnson's a different man on the pitch – it's like he becomes a kid again,' Dilshan grinned.

'I can't believe that Ryan is so shy on the pitch when his dad plays like that,' I said.

'Well, Johnson is very religious and a very strict Seventh Day Adventist. He won't drink or smoke or leave the house on Saturday – not even for a game of football. He has brought Ryan up that way so he doesn't have any natural aggression.'

Dilshan's dad, Vasantha, had also turned up to watch and explained that he would be back playing again soon but was injured. Despite being naturally left-footed, he had taught himself to play with his right foot after suffering a serious injury. I would get used to stories like theirs throughout the football community. Without any trusted medical care any injury would have to be bypassed rather than fixed. Most foreigners on the island take out insurance cover that will pay to fly them off if they need an operation. Locals have to make do with the under-equipped and much maligned Pohnpei State Hospital.

As I sat down to take my boots off I caught sight of a creased piece of paper on the ground with a picture of someone in a Yeovil shirt on it. I unfolded it with a stab of panic. It was a printout of our story from the *Sun*: 'Brits to Coach "Worst Ever Side"'. I went bright red. The players were talking in Pohnpeian and I was certain they were spitting abuse at me. The look on my face must have been pained enough to bring a worried Dilshan over.

'Have the players seen this?' I asked, showing him the paper.

'Oh, um, yes they did,' Dilshan said. 'One of the International FC players, Jeff, printed it out and showed it to them before you came back.'

I felt a wave of nausea. When I gave my little speech about setting up a league they had probably been looking at me with hatred rather than support. Why hadn't they let on? Were they planning their revenge?

'It's OK, most of them just laughed it off,' Dilshan said. 'They know you're here to help. Joseph was the only one who got really angry. He tore the page up on the spot.'

I had never wanted to turn Pohnpei into a joke, but I feared that was exactly what I had done. All the positivity that had built up over the course of the last forty-eight hours of getting to know the players on the island seemed to evaporate. I was a long way from home, trying to earn the respect of a community that had good reason to hate me before they had ever met me. I was worried I might have lost the confidence of the players before I'd even had a chance to start.

5

MAD DOGS AND AN ENGLISHMAN

All my instincts told me to run, but that was the one thing I had been told not to do. I continued slowly backing away, but the larger dog was still barking wildly and advancing menacingly. I knew that I was supposed either to maintain eye contact or to avoid it completely. I cursed myself for not being able to remember which. I could see the lights of my hotel from where I was, just a hundred metres away, but my short cut back from the Telecom Centre had backfired badly when I had unwittingly aggravated a gang of four dogs. In the daytime heat they can barely be bothered to scratch themselves, but at night they come alive and are a wholly different proposition.

Remembering a nugget of advice I had been given by Charles Musana, I slowly bent down and pretended to pick up a rock. Intrigued, the dogs fell silent. I mimed throwing my pretend rock, at the same time backing further away. The dogs recoiled but seemed less than impressed once it became clear I had been bluffing. They began to advance again, so I pulled the same trick. To my immense relief, it worked again. Slowly but surely I was able to back off all the way to my room, whereupon the dogs lost interest and went in search of another target. I slammed the door and slowly my heart rate returned to normal.

After a few drinks with Dilshan at the Rusty Anchor I had decided to give Lizzie a call during her lunch break at work, looking to compensate for a run of terrible connections during conversations. We'd had another call in which every word had to be repeated and the delay meant we'd talk over each other. I had been trying to phone my brother every few days as I knew his wife Emily was about to go into labour. I was the last person in the family to celebrate the birth of my nephew Kit and knew that he would be a couple of months old by the time I met him. I'd completely stopped checking the Bristol City scores. For the first week or so I had worked out the time difference and stayed up until 3 a.m. refreshing the live-match feed, but after a couple of weeks I had lost track of who we were playing. It was partly the anti-social hours, partly the poor quality and very expensive internet connection but mostly a sense of increasing disconnectedness from the outside world. Pohnpeians regard their island as the universe and I was starting to sense that was the only possible way to live here and stay sane.

The quest to find enough teams for a league had started promisingly and I had high hopes for the next stop – the College of Micronesia. Where better to find a football team than a college containing a huge pool of young men? In Pohnpei students received very generous grants from the US government simply to stay in education, so there was never a shortage of applicants for courses. A match was scheduled for that afternoon, and Dilshan had offered to take me.

The College of Micronesia's main campus in Pohnpei is near the island's administrative capital, Palikir. Playing Pohnpei's Canberra to Kolonia's Sydney, Palikir is merely two roads of office buildings. As we climbed the hill leading to the campus, Dilshan revealed that his dad Vasantha ran football games on the COM campus, where he worked in the registration office and acted as a coach to the players there. I was excited at the idea of seeing another football pitch on Pohnpei. Recently, the COM team had even come to PICS Field to play the Pit Bulls.

'It was a good challenge, but we won, of course,' Dilshan said with evident relish at prevailing in the Senarathgoda family rivalry.

A full eleven-a-side match was taking place and the whoops of excitement suggested that the players were enjoying it. The grass was much shorter than at PICS and looked well maintained, but there was a significant slope. I recognised a couple of players, including the distinctive bulky frame of Alika in goal. They were using the equipment we had brought over on the first trip and looked very professional in Yeovil and Norwich kits. Vasantha gave us a wave, then went back to refereeing.

As I scanned the pitch, I was surprised to see two huge and powerful defenders – one playing for each side. The game often descended into head tennis between the two six-footers, who were head and shoulders above not only everyone else on the pitch, but also all the other players I had seen on the island. I had been concerned about the lack of commanding centre backs in Pohnpei. Any team worth its salt has at least one powerhouse to man the defence – a bruiser that nobody wants to play against – but I hadn't seen anyone on the island so far to fit that bill. The average height of locals was comfortably under six-foot and most of the talented players at PICS were closer to five foot than six, but now I was looking at two monsters in island terms. And better still, they both seemed to have a good level of skill and positioning. Dilshan could see exactly what I was thinking.

'The tallest player is Tom Mawi,' he said. 'He has Fijian parents but he's lived here for years. He's always juggling basketball and football commitments. I know he'd play football more if he could, but he can't find boots to fit him. His feet are size fourteen – they are probably the biggest on the island!'

Sure enough, Tom was playing in bare feet. If that was the only obstacle, I felt sure we would overcome it. I'd get Tom some boots and lure him away from basketball. This man was going to be our central defensive rock whether he liked it or not.

'Maybe we should go and chat to him?' I suggested.

'Tom's a great guy and I know him quite well,' Dilshan explained. 'But he doesn't say much. In fact he barely ever says anything unless he knows you really well.'

The other tall defender was more of a mystery. We asked Vasantha at half-time who he was. 'That's Denson. He's good, eh? He doesn't go to COM but when he's around he comes and plays so we can balance out the advantage of Tom. I think he's a taxi driver.'

Another player had come to my attention, cut from a completely different cloth. Rodrigo Matamba was a tiny, tricky winger. While we watched he scored once, hit the bar once and forced a superb diving save from Alika. He looked about fifteen but Vasantha told us he was eighteen. Rodrigo was a cousin of Bob and Robert but bore very little resemblance to them in looks or personality. A devout Jehovah's Witness, Rodrigo was extremely quiet and mild-mannered and Vasantha told us that Rodrigo had barely uttered a word to him in all the years he had known him.

'We will definitely put a team together for the league,' Vasantha declared. 'This time I think we can even beat the Pit Bulls!'

We headed back to Kolonia in a positive frame of mind. Just as we were reaching home, we came across Bob Paul with two young boys I presumed to be his sons.

'Hey, I want to talk to you,' he shouted in his distinctive tone. I always struggled to understand Bob and was glad to have Dilshan there as a translator. Bob told us that he had started a team which he wanted to enter into the league, and asked us to come and see them in action. We waited at Bob's house while he dropped off the kids. I'd noticed the house that Bob and Robert shared when I was walking around Kolonia: it was hard to miss, being painted red, blue and white. As we sat outside watching a swarm of children playing a crude form of baseball with a stick and a stone I noticed with a jolt the main room of the house was a mausoleum, immaculately kept and decked with fresh flowers.

'Bob and Robert's brother was killed in Iraq,' Dilshan told me. 'The US embassy built them the house on the condition that they keep this mausoleum in perfect condition. Someone comes and checks on it every month or so.'

Bob returned wearing a T-shirt saying 'Back from Iraq' and broke the sombre mood in the car. 'Come on, gay boys, let's go for a cruise,' he laughed. 'Off to the jungle to see my Island Warriors.'

Bob directed us down an overgrown jungle road. He certainly knew how to talk the talk and had been telling us we would be blown away by his 'Spartans'. 'When we're playing, you will think there are three hundred of us,' he said three or four times before changing tack and asking us if he could borrow some cones, bibs and a ball. Bob's habit of repeating himself helped my bid to understand him.

Eventually, he made us stop at a seemingly arbitrary point in a small jungle clearing. Three huge, powerful men emerged from the undergrowth, each with a machete in his hand. I extended my own, fearing it might be chopped off, but the Island Warriors shook it warmly. The players wanted to know when they could get started. We told them it would be soon, and since there wasn't much more to say, we returned to the car.

'I hear you met one of our other players today,' Bob said with a crooked smile. 'Denson told me you were up at COM. He's our big man.'

I woke up on a beautiful bright Sunday morning covered in fresh mosquito bites but feeling positive. I had been invited to lunch by Ryan's dad Johnson at his house in the compound of the Seventh Day Adventist School: my next target.

Seventh Day Adventism is one of the primary religions in Pohnpei. I didn't know much about it before I arrived there but learned from Dilshan that his entire family was SDA. Though I was fairly ignorant of SDA ideology, I gathered from snippets of conversation on the football pitch that drinking and smoking were strictly forbidden and that, as in Judaism, the Sabbath runs from Friday sundown to Saturday sundown: a significant obstacle for Saturday football.

Johnson had recently taken over the running of the school, regarded as the best on the island, and, like most of the teachers, he lived inside the school gates. Many players in the International FC team were young volunteer teachers from Australia and the USA who had come to Pohnpei on a single-year placement. Johnson would corral these potential athletes into playing and deliver them to games in his big red truck.

In the last few meetings between International FC and the

Island Pit Bulls there had actually been too many International players. Dilshan had mentioned to Johnson that the SDA should have its own team and he had responded positively. We planned to discuss it over lunch. I was also fascinated to see more of Johnson's son Ryan in his domestic environment.

Dilshan led the way up the stairs and we were greeted at the door by Johnson wearing a 1995 AC Milan shirt. Despite his brutal on-field reputation, Johnson was a jovial figure off the pitch and a smile rarely left his face. Johnson had been a close friend of Charles Musana and the two men had kept football running throughout the 1990s, engineering games at PICS and treating them like Cup Finals regardless of the turnout.

Johnson led us into his living room, where I was introduced to his wife Rupa, Dilshan's mum Devanesam and a string of SDA volunteer teachers who were all clean-shaven, blond and earnest. Sitting quietly on the other side of the room was Ryan with his sister Judelle. He nodded in greeting and went back to watching the TV, which was tuned to a Christian channel. Dilshan's dad Vasantha was hard at work in the kitchen, although I could see on the table four huge bowls of curry that he had already produced and enough rice to feed most of the island. Since arriving in Pohnpei I had never seen so much food in any one place; I felt a little overawed.

'We could definitely make a team for SDA, you know,' Johnson was saying to Dilshan. 'I could make sure we had at least eleven for every game. You guys would play soccer, wouldn't you?' the head teacher asked the SDA volunteers.

There was a murmur of assent. It was hard to gauge the genuine level of enthusiasm.

'I played quite a lot in Australia,' one volunteer piped up.

'Sure, if we're not surfing we'll definitely play,' another said, not understanding that Johnson hadn't really asked a question so much as issued an order.

'How about you, Ryan; you can play for SDA?' Johnson asked.

'I'm a Pit Bull,' Ryan said quietly, earning a cheer and a slap on the back from Dilshan. Ryan had been even more withdrawn than usual. It was only when Dilshan encouraged him that he spoke. He clearly looked up to his older cousin and he seemed to grow in confidence after Dilshan's pat on the back.

'In any case, we'll have eleven,' Johnson said. 'If only I could get this many people to play cricket.'

Like most Sri Lankans, Johnson loved cricket. He fondly recalled his abortive attempts to explain the game to Charles Musana. 'In ten years I never managed to get him to understand the rules,' he laughed. 'I think he still believes LBW is a kind of disease!'

Two hours later we left the SDA compound a team stronger and a stone heavier. Johnson and his family had refused to start eating until we were on our third plate. I hadn't needed much encouragement and had eaten more in that sitting than in the whole of the previous week. That was Dilshan's fault. He barely ever seemed to eat anything. Maybe it was the temperature or the fact that we were always together, but I'd started to follow suit. Every few days we'd go and get a fishburger from Ocean View – they became so accustomed to us that they would start preparing the food as they saw Dilshan's car pull up in the car park – or we'd visit Angie's – Pohnpei's answer to McDonald's and the butt of local jokes as its fast food would take half an hour to arrive. Anyway, by the time we'd reached Johnson's house, I'd been well up for a blowout.

Dilshan lived with his parents in a two-bedroom apartment. His neighbours were almost all from the Philippines and all seemed to have at least five deafeningly loud children. As a child in Sri Lanka,

Dilshan had been an excellent cricketer and could have represented his country, but when his family moved to Pohnpei, football became his passion. Dreaming of playing professionally, he moved to the Philippines and did well in a tough league, but his family duties pulled him back to Pohnpei, where he had tried to create opponents for himself. Every time I arrived at Dilshan's house his mum would immediately appear and whip up some food for us, regardless of our protests. She had reached the accurate conclusion that I wouldn't be able to afford to eat well on Pohnpei and refused to let us leave the house for football until we had managed a meal. Despite her hospitality I had certainly lost weight and Dilshan enjoyed reminding me of how 'fat' I'd been when I'd first arrived. I would respond by telling him he weighed less than a schoolgirl: Dilshan was certainly in good shape but he was almost gaunt and in England would be told to bulk up if he wanted to play football at a high level.

Two weeks in, I had a phone call from Jim Tobin. The Olympic Committee chief had just returned to the island after a trip to the US and had heard talk of a league. He was very excited and called me to his office for a meeting. 'Any time tomorrow,' he said. 'Just make sure you call first.'

The next day was oppressively hot and by the time I had walked the quarter-mile to Jim's office I was sweating. Puddles of water in the street served as evidence that there had been a storm in the night. As I entered the Olympic Committee office I was greeted warmly by Lestly, Jim's secretary, who was typing with one hand, signing documents with the other and, had she had a third, it would doubtless have been engaged in another pressing task. It was the first time in Pohnpei I had seen anyone working that hard.

Jim rose and vigorously shook my hand. 'Welcome back,' he boomed in a mock-cockney accent. The power of the big man's handshake reminded me not to get on the wrong side of him, but fortunately Jim was buzzing with enthusiasm.

'I can't wait for the start of the league,' he beamed. 'If it works out then we can really push for more funding for football. I took a risk backing football because the guys behind the other sports see it as a rival, but I feel you're going to prove me right.'

Technically, Jim wasn't supposed to support us at all. In order to qualify for National Olympic Committee funding, as with FIFA, we would have to be active on all Micronesian islands, but Jim explained that he saw our work in Pohnpei as a pilot project. If it worked we could use the momentum to go to Yap, Chuuk and Kosrae, but at this stage our resources were so limited that to try a four-state scheme would spread us far too thin.

'How many teams will you have?'

'So far, five. International FC, the Island Pit Bulls, COM, the Island Warriors and an SDA team have all committed,' I said. 'We want to start the league in a week's time, but we'll need to get the pitch in order.'

'How are you getting around?' Jim asked.

'On foot, mostly, but Dilshan has been really good about giving me lifts.'

'I'm not strictly allowed to do this because we've got a delegation coming in from Fiji tomorrow, but why don't you take the Olympic Committee car,' Jim said, tossing the keys to me over the desk. 'I'll get grief for this, but if you want to get something done then you've got to look after your guys.'

I descended the steps and looked for the FSM NOC's Kia. Like most cars on the island it had seen its fair share of scrapes: the steering wheel was cracked and oozed ants and it always smelt a little of damp. With the exception of the big cars that wealthy Americans had shipped over when they moved in, the cars on Pohnpei resembled a boxcar rally. Most had been imported second hand from Japan and Korea where their previous owners had been forced to sell them by environmental laws banning vehicles over a certain age. These long-suffering vehicles didn't enjoy a peaceful retirement on the pothole-ridden roads on Pohnpei.

The Committee's Kia was pretty good by local standards and I certainly wasn't complaining. I had only one problem: I couldn't drive. I'd had a few lessons here and there back in the UK, but the cost had always prevented me from getting anywhere near a licence. In any Western country I would have politely refused Jim's offer, but on an island where the average driving speed was 20 mph and most people openly chewed betel nut while driving, I felt that I was just about as qualified as anyone. Besides, it was an automatic, which is as hard to drive as a go-kart. Even so, my first few days behind the wheel were nervy and I marked myself out as a foreigner by failing to steer wide of the endless string of potholes on the major roads.

Goalkeeper Charles immediately saw through me. 'I seen that guy drive,' he laughed, pointing at me before a kickaround at PICS Field. 'He looks so nervous, man, I was thinking: He don't know how to drive!' I'd had to let Dilshan in on my secret, as I'd needed him to reverse out of a tight parking space on my first day in charge of the Kia. He'd been very understanding and even complimented my progress a few days later when I'd taken the wheel on our weekly fishburger trip by insisting he felt 'much less terrified'.

We had enough teams for a league, albeit a rather small one, the support of the Olympic Committee and even a company car, but just as everything seemed to be on track, I received a call from Steve Finnen, the captain of International FC, who worriedly informed me that an unexpectedly large number of his players had joined Johnson's SDA team, and he was struggling to field eleven bodies. This was a serious blow. We had hoped to get the league started in three days' time and we badly needed International FC to be in it. In trying to strengthen the league with the addition of an SDA team, we feared we might have actually weakened it.

It was time for a recruitment drive. Over a beer in the Rusty Anchor Dilshan and I started to list any foreign groups on the island who could provide a player. Like me, most foreigners had arrived through unorthodox means. Some had decided to throw in sensible jobs in the US or Europe to travel and had never returned. Others had married Micronesians abroad and come back to settle down with the in-laws. But most foreigners find Pohnpei as volunteers. There were various volunteer organisations such as World Teach and the Peace Corps, but their personnel were often put in accommodation in the remote villages on the other side of the island. We worked out that we needed athletic foreigners based nearby – which was how we came up with the idea of becoming the first people ever to cold-call a Mormon church.

There was a strong community of Mormons on the island who worshipped in the bleached white Church of Jesus Christ of Latter-Day Saints on top of a hill on the outskirts of Kolonia. Every now and again we would see young American Mormon volunteers cycling around looking extremely uncomfortable in their incongruously formal uniform of black trousers, white shirt and black tie. However unsuitable their attire, they seemed to get results and the Mormon church had a significant Pohnpeian following. Dilshan and I raised a toast to the Mormons – and then got in some more beers.

The next morning, still smelling of beer, we knocked on the door of the volunteer accommodation building in the Mormon compound. The door opened to reveal Elders Hatch and Thoms, two disconcertingly young American lads who had taken advantage of the privacy of their hut to remove almost all of their cumbersome uniforms. A little too much was on show for our comfort, but, not to be deterred from our mission, we were heartened to see that they barely had an inch of fat between them. We briefly explained who we are and asked whether either elder would like to take part in our football league.

'When we're on a mission we're not allowed to do anything but preach the word of God,' the slightly older elder explained while the other made a belated attempt to salvage his reputation by pulling some clothes on.

Although the role reversal had clearly put them on the back foot, we appeared to be preaching to the inconvertible. However, I had an ace up my sleeve.

'That's odd, because we saw you playing flag American football by Spanish Wall last week.' There was always a group of Mormons down there on Thursdays.

The now-clothed younger elder could only field this one in an inaudible mumble, possibly claiming that flag football is in the Book of Mormon somewhere.

'I used to play soccer a lot in the US at quite a good level. I really miss it, but our work comes first,' the older elder insisted.

Football was a no-go, then. As we turned to leave, Elder Thoms took an audacious shot at getting us to convert, inviting us to their

Sunday service. We politely refused. Our away day with the Mormons had ended in an honourable goalless draw.

Our final effort to drum up support for the league was to deliver a press release to the *Kaselehlie Press* – the sole window into current affairs for the local population in which Matt and I had advertised during our first visit to Pohnpei. We knocked on the door of the paper's offices and entered to see a dog sitting non-plussed at a drum kit in the middle of the room. Behind a small partition was Bill Jaynes, the editor and more or less the paper's sole journalist, reading through an article with his feet up on the desk. Bill greeted us warmly and responded to my backwards glance at his musical dog by revealing himself to be a member of Wetter Than Seattle. His son was actually the drummer, while Bill played lead guitar.

'So, the famous Mr Watson is back on Pohnpei,' the tall grey-haired editor said with a grin. 'I've been reading all about you and "the worst team in the world".'

Dilshan laughed but I squirmed and prepared for some abuse, even though it seemed unlikely to come from someone as pleasant as Bill.

'I have Google alerts set up on my computer, so every time a story gets printed that mentions Pohnpei, I get an email. My inbox was full for days!'

Embarrassed, I muttered an explanation. We had needed publicity to get funding but it had got out of hand. The usual stuff.

'Hey, don't worry,' Bill laughed. 'At first I thought you might be a real dick, but I figured, let's wait and see. If you come back here then your heart's probably in the right place.'

Bill happily accepted our press release and wished us all the best for the league, telling us to bring our match reports to him.

We carefully drew up a fixture list for the first weekend and sat back with a great feeling of satisfaction.

WEEK 1
Island Pit Bulls v. Island Warriors
COM v. International FC

The next day we planned to mark out the PICS Field pitch for the first time. We wanted everything to look professional for the big kick-off and had only twenty-four hours to do it. Our resources were a far cry from those in England. Without a machine to line the pitch, we had collected the next best thing: two buckets of paint, some pieces of string and two rollers (the kind you would use to paint your front room). The day we had chosen to mark the pitch was scalding hot, even by Pohnpei standards. A group of the most committed Pit Bulls had turned up: the usual suspects, Ryan, Joseph, Rocky and Charles. We were also joined by Jason, an International FC player who worked at the US embassy. He happened to mention that he had been a referee back in the US and knew all the pitch dimensions. Under his direction we laboriously measured the lengths of the penalty boxes and the halfway line with the string. At the same time a group of Pit Bulls used an old lawn-mower borrowed from Johnson, and a great deal of elbow grease, to cut the grass.

We began work at 8 a.m. and by midday the sun was so hot that even the locals were starting to complain. I had applied a whole bottle of suntan lotion before we left in the morning but I could feel it dripping off as I sweated. We were running out of paint and had to use a dotted line on one side of the pitch, but it looked better than anyone could remember. I wish the same could have been said about me. By the time I got home I was so sunburned that I didn't recognise my reflection. My arms were aching and I felt sick. I knew that I had to be there the next morning to referee the opening game between the Island Pit Bulls and Bob Paul's new Island Warriors, but for now all I could do was lie in a darkened room and curse my pale Celtic colouring.

I was there for the opener with my blistering skin covered as best I could. A frantic search for after-sun lotion had been fruitless as shop attendants struggled to understand the concept behind the product I wanted. Dilshan was pumped up and all his Pit Bulls were at PICS Field on time in their Yeovil Town shirts, except for Charles and Joseph who were their customary fifteen minutes late. Bob's Island Warriors showed up in theatrical fashion, pulling up in one big truck and jumping down from the back all dressed in black. However, the 'Spartans' of the Island Warriors weren't exactly what had been advertised. Only one of the imposing machete-wielding figures from the jungle was there and the rest of the team were barely in their teens. Bob grinned. The possibility of a heavy defeat didn't seem to be as important to him as having pulled the wool over our eyes. A small crowd of intrigued spectators gathered as Pohnpeian football entered a new era. Bob physically pushed six 'men' off the field to leave nine. I called two back on and we were ready to kick off.

The game was a walkover. The Pit Bulls, led by Dilshan, won 9–2, with the captain scoring four, but Bob impressed and managed to breach their defence twice. It was the first time I'd seen genuine promise in Bob. His rival Joseph was equally potent for the Pit

Bulls, scoring twice from outside the box. While it was clear the Warriors hadn't played much organised football, one player stood out: the mysterious defender with huge biceps covered in tattoos who we'd seen playing at COM had a great eye for the game. Denson Fairfield was clearly one to watch.

My own first full competitive game as a player on PICS was a humbling experience. I'd cried off from the match against COM, but a week on and my sunburn had actually worsened. My arms were covered in sores where the dead skin had peeled, exposing raw flesh underneath. I was in a lot of pain and had set aside my financial qualms and gone to a doctor, who had prescribed me some pills called Keflex. Dilshan laughed as I collected them.

'Whatever's wrong with you, they always give you Keflex,' he told me. 'I'm taking them now for an ankle pain, my mum's taking them and so is my dad. They're the only pill they give here.'

Foolishly I decided I would still play for International FC against the Pit Bulls on the second week of the league. Against all the odds, we managed to field eleven men, including an unfamiliar defensive pairing that no one recognised comprising a tall Croatian with a shaved head and a chubby American. Even when the pair helpfully reminded us we had approached them in the Rusty Anchor days before, we had no memory of it. Unable to run and feeling woozy, I decided I would play in goal.

After five minutes the heavens opened in typical Pohnpeian style. The lines visibly started to wash off the pitch and pools of water accumulated within seconds. Dilshan played a through ball, which I ran out to get. I had loads of time until the ball sunk deep into a puddle and stopped. By the time I reached it, Ryan had dinked it over me into the net. To make matters worse I had skidded out face first and was now covered head to toe in mud. I trudged back to my line, where I saw a man wearing glasses and an Arsenal shirt shaking his head.

'Come on, geezer, this isn't what I expect from England!' he crowed in a London accent.

I was pretty sure I was hallucinating.

'Don't want to put you off, like, but thought I'd say hello. I'm Steve from Shepherd's Bush. You're from Hammersmith, aren't you? Just down the road. We should go for a pint when you get a chance.'

Distracted by a Dilshan shot fizzing just wide of the post, I didn't notice Steve disappear as quickly as he had arrived. My bafflement at meeting a man from Shepherd's Bush on an island 8,000 miles from home couldn't excuse the five other goals that flew past me during that game. The Pit Bulls had shown themselves to be a class above. I just hoped they didn't think I was nothing more than a bumbling goalkeeper.

Back at the hotel, after a long shower I looked at the crumpled checklist Matt and I had created all those weeks ago. 1. Get sponsor. There hadn't been much progress on that front. 2. Set up league. That could be ticked off. 3. Pick Pohnpei team. That was our next task.

I had now seen each of the teams play at least once and had been encouraged by the level of talent. Sitting in the Ocean View Hotel with Dilshan, knocking back a Corona as we talked about the selection, I was already excited by our striking line and felt we could build a good team. Dilshan would be the playmaker, Ryan and Joseph could be a lethal pairing up front if we could get Ryan to be a little more physical. We now had two big men in defence in Tom Mawi and Denson Fairfield, and Rocky and Roger were very capable wing-backs. What worried me most was the lack of a defensive midfielder.

'Trust me, I know a couple of guys who could play for Pohnpei but you might not have seen the best of them yet,' Dilshan said.

We had a list of players we both agreed should be in a Pohnpei team. Dilshan wanted to bring in two other wild cards and I was happy to bow to his greater knowledge of the local talent pool. The league still had weeks to run, but I had seen what I needed to see. It was time to start building a Pohnpei team.

6

TEAM POHNPEI

Boils: A **boil**, also called a **furuncle**, is a deep **folliculitis**, infection of the hair follicle. It is almost always caused by infection by the bacterium *Staphylococcus aureus*, resulting in a painful swollen area on the skin caused by an accumulation of pus and dead tissue.

There was no doubt about it: I had boils. I had always thought of boils in the same vein as consumption or whooping cough, as something a character in a Dickens novel might get. Nonetheless it was 2010 and I was being tormented by a handful of unsightly and surprisingly painful lumps that would eventually burst at the most inopportune moment. The cream of Pohnpei's medical professionals had prodded and poked the angry red blobs but had labelled them 'unlucky' and insisted I take it easy and wait for them to run their course. Everything had gone downhill since I'd allowed myself to get irredeemably sunburned while marking out the pitch for the inaugural league match. I was relieved that there was work to do to distract me from the boils, not just on the pitch but at an administrative level too.

As we started building a Pohnpei team, it stood to reason that we needed to design a kit, even though this would merely be a theoretical gesture until I was back in England and could find someone capable of making it. There was only one man who could help me with such a crucial task: the same man who had spent four hours rating Spanish Segunda División shirts with me when I should have been working for *Football Italia*. I'd been in regular email contact with Matt all through my time in Pohnpei and it was nice to have a joint mission again. Separated by thousands of miles, we trawled through website after website, analysing styles and designs and rating them exhaustively before finally selecting the new Pohnpei strip. We opted for a sleek Adidas shirt in deep blue with white sleeves, to echo the colours of the Pohnpei flag. We looked at the preview image and agreed that it was a thing of beauty. The lack of a sponsor still loomed large, but I had sent out emails to friends and to friends of friends asking for small dona-tions and was surprised when my appeal yielded sufficient funds to kit out our team.

Dilshan and I had set a date for our first Pohnpei State training session and sent out the invites to the players who had caught our eye. I slept poorly the night before the session. I had spent the last few months happily giving interviews as the Pohnpei coach, writing emails as the Pohnpei coach, being introduced to people as the Pohnpei coach, but I hadn't really coached anyone yet. In fact, I had never formally coached anyone at anything, ever. I spent hours tossing and turning, running through training routines in my head and trying to work out which of the millions of problems that could arise would arise.

The morning of the big day was bright but pleasingly temper-ate. In my broken sleep I had a dream where I had no cones and had to mark out areas with toads. I checked the boot of the car and breathed a sigh of relief to find the cones exactly where I had left them. The session wasn't until 4 p.m. and the hours passed agonisingly slowly. I filled my time writing increasingly elaborate plans, binning them and writing new ones. Every hour or so I phoned Dilshan to make sure he had told everyone what time to turn up. At the end of our fourth conversation he told me to stop calling him and that he would see me at the pitch. Adrenaline coursed through my veins. Ever since I'd arrived I had been feeling something of a fraud, calling myself a coach before I had actually begun coaching, and it had grown to become a huge nagging worry. Finally, I was going to get that monkey off my back – but there was also a fair amount of pressure, for this was the moment I had been visualising since Matt and I had first visited the island seven months earlier. I checked the equipment in my car for the umpteenth time and set off for PICS Field with an hour to spare. I had overestimated the level of traffic in Kolonia, where three cars is considered a jam, so I reached the pitch forty-five minutes before our start time. Unsurprisingly, nobody was there. I'd even arrived before Rocky.

I sat in the car and waited as dark clouds began to gather overhead and flecks of rain hit the windscreen. Having seen my men playing through flash floods, I knew a drop of rain wouldn't bother the Pohnpei State hardcore, but I wasn't delighted at the idea of trying to conduct my maiden training session in a downpour.

When 4 p.m. did arrive, there wasn't a single player in sight, but the rain had eased to a steady drizzle.

The first arrivals were a mere five minutes late – positively early by Pohnpeian standards – but I struggled to recognise them. They were the two wild-card players that Dilshan had vouched for – Marvin and Nick. I had seen them play in the game up at the College of Micronesia. Marvin had looked pretty good on the wing, but I couldn't remember Nick at all. A baby-faced twenty-year-old, Marvin was a committed Mormon who never joined his fellow players on nights out but was more than happy to join in with off-field banter. Marvin's father had been a celebrated athlete on Pohnpei but died in his prime in mysterious circumstances. Many locals insist he was the victim of black magic, some kind of voodoo curse, and though keen to know more, I knew I could never ask Marvin about it. As we made small talk, I learned that Marvin had travelled a considerable distance to be there and had still beaten most of his new teammates.

'I'm very excited, Coach,' Marvin said softly. 'We're going to be a proper team for Pohnpei. I have always loved football since Charles Musana taught me to play when I was six.'

In contrast, the other wild card, Nick, had been playing football for only a matter of weeks. Dilshan had taken him under his wing and Nick had come on remarkably quickly. I doubted that Nick would make the grade, but I enjoyed talking to him: he was extremely well spoken and clearly intelligent.

'I'm studying medicine,' he told me. 'I find that I can study football in a similar way and I'm picking up the techniques and the tactics by reading and watching games.'

The conversation was interrupted by a car horn and a taxi pulled up, driven by Denson Fairfield, the tall, powerful defender we had seen playing at COM.

Denson wound down the window. 'Hey, Coach, did I come third?' He grinned as if he had won a medal. 'The rest of these guys are on island time, but they'll be here. I saw Joseph and Charles on the way.'

As Denson got out of his battered yellow taxi, I realised with a start that there was somebody in the back seat. The stranger was a few stone overweight and chewing methodically on betel nut, pausing occasionally to spit the foul red juice into a Coke can. He certainly wasn't a footballer. 'That's my fare,' Denson explained, catching me staring. 'He's going to Nett, so I'll drop him off when I go back after training.' Denson seemed so unconcerned at leaving a paying customer in his cab for the best part of two hours that I decided to let it lie. I was still fretting about the lack of players, but chatting to Denson was a nice distraction. He spoke perfect English with a mixed American-Micronesian accent; he revealed that this was because he had been brought up in Guam, which I had been told many times has excellent footballing facilities. Denson had been a keen footballer there and, as I was later to discover, had played for several years as a goalkeeper, which went some way towards explaining the defender's seemingly natural eye for the game that first caused us to pick him for the Pohnpei squad.

'I can help translate for the guys who don't speak English so well,' Denson offered. 'Some of the players will tell you if they don't understand but most of them will be too shy.'

Of the fifteen players expected to turn up, I knew that at least three generally struggled to understand me and two were clearly baffled by most of what I said. The player I felt the least natural connection with was Micah, who had never really warmed to me. A gifted athlete, Micah had excelled on the right wing for the Island Pit Bulls in what we had now dubbed the Pohnpei Premier League, but his attitude had been less than exemplary. On several occasions Micah had turned up late, despite living directly behind PICS Field – although he was not alone in bad timekeeping. Worse, he often turned up stoned or drunk and once he didn't bother to come at all. Dilshan had told me that Micah was also a talented basketball player and might be more committed to the rival sport. I was glad to have Denson to act as a middle man, translating what I said to those who struggled.

By the time I returned from laying down the cones, most of the players had arrived. Rocky was doing his customary laps of the running track, but at a quicker pace as if to make up for his relative lateness, and Bob and Robert turned up with their younger cousin Rodrigo trailing by a few hundred metres like a schoolboy trying to avoid his friends seeing his dad drop him off at the gates. It was now 4.30 and Dilshan's car pulled up. The captain had driven around Kolonia rounding up the stragglers and finally we had a full complement. I started with a simple warm-up and stretch routine, and it became obvious that the players had never been introduced to the idea of warming up. I had to demonstrate running with high knees three times and a short spell of sidestepping left three men on the ground and the rest roaring with laughter.

I had drafted a simple session. In truth, parts of it looked more like a school PE lesson than an international team at work, but it was essential to see exactly how firm the basics were before I introduced anything more complicated. When we did start doing a relatively complex crossing drill, I was astonished to find that the players acquitted themselves much better than they had during the simple run-and-pass exercise that had resulted in so much head scratching and numerous balls rolling onto the running track. The players were certainly paying attention to what I was saying and watched demonstrations eagerly. I found that it helped to give instructions twice, however ridiculous it sounded. During games players always shouted: 'cornercorner' or 'passpass', and repetition seemed to make English sound more like Pohnpeian: a singsong, rhyming language. Those who looked blank while I was talking usually came to life when Denson offered a Pohnpeian version.

Whenever I paused to change the layout of the cones or grab a set of bibs, the players gave in to their innate urge to kick a football towards a goal and by the time I'd returned the majority of them were scampering after their wayward efforts. For the first time I fully empathised with the football coaches and PE teachers I had exasperated during my childhood. The exception was Nick Santiago, Dilshan's wild-card medical student. Now I could see why Dilshan had drafted him in: I struggled to believe Nick had only recently been introduced to football. His eye for the game was exceptional, his passing excellent, and although he was average height for a Pohnpeian, he always seemed to come out on top in 50–50 challenges. Dilshan had been moulding him to play alongside him in midfield and it seemed that we had the all-important foil for Dilshan: Nick would be our holding midfielder.

I finished the session with static stretches, most of which were completely new to the players – which possibly explained the awesome arsenal of long-standing injuries the group reported to me over the course of training. As soon as we completed the stretches a group of players, led by Micah, hurried off with a cursory nod by way of salutation. Rocky, on the other hand, hadn't quenched his thirst for physical activity and headed off to the running track, cutting a solitary figure as he ran laps in the dying sun.

Dilshan wasn't finished yet; he gathered up all the balls and lined them up about twenty yards from goal. He hit them one by one, most of them fizzing into the corners but occasionally lifting one over the top and into the jungle the other side of the running track. I stayed with him, trying to help with the angle of contact and taking on the unenviable role of defensive wall. Dilshan was clearly the best player on the island but he was desperate to improve, a quality that I admired. After his fifteenth lap, Rocky came and doubled the width of our wall, making a big show of covering his crotch with his hands. He didn't even seem out of breath. When it was too dark to see, we went our separate ways. As I drove home, the heavens opened and I allowed myself a smile of relief and satisfaction. The Pohnpeians clearly had a lot to learn about the tactical side of the game but overall things had gone much more smoothly than I had anticipated. I tried not to wonder what the players thought of my coaching credentials or how I would have done without Denson translating my instructions into Pohnpeian and snapping at anyone whose attention wavered: instead I dwelt on the positives. I felt I had finally truly become a coach and dared to believe for the first time that I could be a leader.

After the hard work on the pitch it was time for some team building and, as ever, that meant drinking – for most of the players at least. Dilshan and I had been talking for some time about a bonding trip to the nearby resort island of Nahlap. Nahlap comprises a few connected idyllic beaches looking out to the deep blue ocean with a dozen or so huts and a chapel where couples often get married. The family that own it offer a ferry service from the mainland and $5 allows you to stay in one of the huts. An overnight stay there would allow our new team to get to know one another.

By chance, the training session had been held on the day that students at the College of Micronesia received their quarterly grants – a day of massive jubilation for most young people on the island. (In fact, it was three weeks after the due date, but the cogs of Micronesian bureaucracy had turned with their habitual sloth.) The majority of our players – indeed, it seemed, the majority of young Pohnpeians – were students, and as I learned more about Pohnpei, the reason for this quickly became apparent: the US government grants provided to Micronesians in education actually dwarf the salaries of many workers in unskilled professions.

Bored of college, our goalkeeper Charles Welson had entered the world of work during my previous trip to Pohnpei. He initially took a job at the airport, but lasted just three days after his boss took exception to him turning up two hours late. Within forty-eight hours he was working in a supermarket, but the job bored him and he left before the week was out. The next week we'd visited Charles in a car parts shop, where he had been manning the till. He'd looked barely conscious, lulled to sleep by a combination of boredom and betel nut. The following Monday he'd returned to college. When we ribbed Charles for his work-shy attitude he shrugged, simply saying: 'What's the point in working hard when you can get paid more spending the day staring at girls?'

Charles's attitude made a lot of sense. Attending college made him eligible for a grant of around $5,500 per annum. I had seen an advert for the role of security guard at the US embassy and the annual salary was just $6,000. I was told that the job market on Pohnpei was very limited as there simply weren't enough positions to fill. Most bright students were able to secure US scholarships to study on the American mainland. However, I was surprised to learn that most of these US-educated graduates return to Pohnpei within five years to settle down, usually in modestly paid, fairly unchallenging government jobs. I couldn't decide whether Pohnpeians return from the supposed Promised Land of the US because they possess a touching family ethic and loyalty to their homeland, or because life on Pohnpei leaves its people unable or unwilling to cope anywhere else.

Dilshan took charge of the preparations for the trip. Every player who was able to paid $10; others pledged to bring rice or chicken or fish. The venture had been amusingly dubbed the 'picnic' by the team. Bob, Robert and Rodrigo went fishing to catch their contribution. We took the money we had collected to the wholesale supermarket and bought crates of vodka, rum and beer. The rest of the money went on renting a truck to allow us to navigate the bumpy dirt tracks outside Kolonia that led to where the Nahlap ferry docked.

Our first stop was PICS Field, which we had set as our collection point. I knew there was no point in rushing, so we turned up exactly on time at 1 p.m. and I was staggered and rather frustrated to see everyone already waiting. It seemed that island time didn't apply to social events. The only absentee was Tom Mawi, our giant Fijian defender, who had told us he had a basketball practice that day. Somehow everyone clambered into the back of the open-backed truck. I was given the honour of riding in the cab. The players, perhaps remembering my boils, were insistent that I shouldn't sit in the sun.

We slowly wound our way to the dock. Every time we turned a corner we risked losing someone as they struggled to hang on. After rounding one particularly sharp bend I heard a siren. A police car had appeared from nowhere and the officer inside was beckoning for us to pull over, concerned at our patently dangerous progress. Apparently most people in Kolonia knew somebody in the police force and in this situation the conversation usually entailed finding out which cousin they had in common with one of your friends, but I was still nervous.

'It's OK,' Dilshan said, reading my expression. 'Alika will deal with it; he knows everyone.'

Sure enough, Alika hopped off the back of the truck and went to talk to the police officer. The officer, who had looked grave, immediately started to grin. The two spoke quickly but the tone was clearly jovial. After a short while, the officer wished us all a good day and returned to his car without so much as inspecting the truck. Alika clambered back on board and yelled, 'Let's go!'

Twenty minutes later we turned down a tiny dirt track and the glistening ocean came into view through the trees. We had arrived at the dock. The 'ferry' to Nahlap turned out to be a small motor boat, so we split into three groups for the picturesque crossing. As soon as we loaded our stuff into a hut overlooking the ocean, the players began to relax and started throwing each other off the pier into the water. Charles was the instigator, sneaking up on Dilshan, Ryan and Marvin, cackling as he launched them off the edge. However, little Ryan was having none of it and after a protracted wrestling match managed to pull Charles in with him. Marvin resurfaced with two crumpled, sodden dollar bills, adding to the squeals of laughter from the rest of the group. Roger needed no coercion to go in the water; he climbed on top of the hut, saluted and then dived from ten feet up, performed a neat somersault and entered the sea without a splash. But Robert, wearing a vest that exposed his sinewy muscled arms and his string of tattoos, wasn't happy. His expressive face was wrinkled in thought and eventually he rose to address the group.

'Coach should talk,' he bellowed. 'Everyone shut up. Coach has to give his speech.'

My insides churned a little. This was just what I didn't want when I finally felt like I was off the clock. The players gave each other knowing looks as they gathered in the hut, not happy to take orders from Robert. I improvised a speech of sorts, but wasn't quite sure what to say. At the risk of tailing off I took the populist option of raising a toast to the Pohnpei State team. The players cheered, but Robert still wasn't happy and was ready to have his say. Bob, whom I gradually learned was the more relaxed of the twins, rolled his eyes as his brother stood to speak.

'We need to be a team,' he said. 'Even on our picnic we must behave like a team. There must be no fighting and we go when our coach tells us to.'

And with that the talking stopped and the drinking began. Most of the players cracked open beers, but Roger politely reminded me that he was 'substance free' and would never drink or do drugs, not even a beer with his mates. It didn't seem to bother him to see his teammates drinking or chewing betel nut up at PICS Field. I suspected that it was too commonplace a sight to elicit a reaction, but Roger also never seemed to take the moral high ground whenever bawdy anecdotes circulated. Ryan and Rodrigo were on the soft drinks too, which I thought showed remarkable maturity for teenagers finally out of their parents' sight.

Charles Musana had warned us on our first trip to Pohnpei that the locals weren't great at holding their drink, so I felt mild trepidation when I saw the speed at which our mountain of alcohol was diminishing. But after having to be the responsible one during matches and at training, I decided it was finally time to act my age and just be one of the lads. Some of the players seemed surprised to see me drinking a beer, but Rocky, Charles and Joseph gave me knowing grins while the usually poker-faced Micah seemed positively delighted.

It was a typically Pohnpeian affair. As the beer flowed the players snacked on cans of luncheon meat, a weird jellied mass that looked and smelt like dog food. Joseph provided the music, courtesy of his phone. Sadly he only had about eight tracks, six of them island versions of US chart R&B songs performed by less gifted vocalists with still more limited lyrics. The seventh and eighth were, bizarrely, John Denver country classics, which Joseph enthusiastically sang along with. The most popular songs in Pohnpei were generally laid-back, with something similar to a reggae beat. I'd frequently noticed that there seemed to be no real awareness of 'new music'. MTV was available on cable, but only the American expats had cable. Most local radio stations, such as Paradise FM, would play songs pretty much at random from any era: there just wasn't a record market to sell to. The State team got their music another way. One player would be sent an MP3 file by a cousin in Guam and all the others would crowd round and listen to it. It could have been recorded last week or in the 1980s, but whichever way it was new on Pohnpei. Bob Marley was very popular with the locals; I wondered how many of them knew he was thirty years dead.

With the sun setting, I was staggering towards our makeshift toilet behind an unoccupied hut when I smelt marijuana. I followed the smoke and found Micah, Rocky and Charles on the floor of a hut passing a joint around. Micah looked as if he had just been caught with a dead body and half-threw the spliff towards Charles, but Charles just smiled and offered it to me. I accepted and the tension was lifted. We were in the same position an hour later when Ryan came running in.

'I didn't want to disturb you, but you should come fast,' he said, not flinching at the smell.

The harmony in the camp had been broken spectacularly. After just three cans of beer, Robert ('... we must behave like a team. There must be no fighting ...') had started acting strangely, trying to pick fights with the younger players. I noticed that Ryan had sensibly kept his distance, but Marvin wasn't so lucky: when he had begun barbecuing the chicken we'd brought, Robert had stormed up to him, thrown it in the sea and told him he was doing it wrong. The mild-mannered teetotaller Marvin hadn't said anything, but Robert had slapped him in the face repeatedly. Luckily, Denson intervened. While Marvin would never speak out against his elder, Denson was old enough and respected enough to oppose him.

As we reached the hut we saw Denson dragging Robert towards the motor boat to leave for the mainland. I turned and made eye contact with Rodrigo, who seemed to give a resigned sigh. I wondered how many times he'd seen this before. 'I'll take him home,' Denson said, unfazed, as Robert made a throat-slitting gesture towards the assembled group. We watched them sail off into the sunset with Denson wrapping the much smaller Robert in a bear hug to prevent him from attacking the boat driver. Shortly after Robert left the island, Bob fell asleep. After revelling in his twin's exile, he had been telling me at length why he was the best striker on the island when he suddenly slumped forward. The mood now felt lighter again. Alika was living up to his reputation as a prolific drinker and for every bottle of beer I drank he had two or three. On the other side of the hut Marvin was happily chatting with Roger, neither of whom had drunk a drop. Rodrigo, on the other hand, looked uncomfortable and kept to himself.

The more he drank, the more English Rocky spoke, and I learned that he had an excellent grasp of the language when he wanted to. Although he didn't have a job, he spent most of his days running errands for his family – which largely involved bringing home enough sakau to keep them in a constant state of intoxication. To do this he was allowed to drive the family's van, a task that required huge concentration, given that it had no brakes. The only way he could stop was by performing a very low-speed crash. It wasn't hard getting Charles's life story out of him. He and Joseph had had a tough upbringing. Their parents died when they were young, leaving them in the care of their grandparents, who had also recently passed away. Now they lived with an uncle: a powerful, easily angered man not to be messed with. I had only seen him once when he came to PICS Field and dragged Joseph off by the neck after he failed to show for a family gathering. However, Charles spoke affectionately of his uncle, who used to be a keen footballer – and who enjoyed teasing Charles and Joseph by saying he could still run rings round them.

While we laughed and joked, Joseph stayed quiet, only occasionally chipping in to ask for more betel nut. He spoke to me just once, to ask where the proper Pohnpei State shirts were. I told him that I needed to pick them up in England.

Suddenly Rocky sat bolt upright.

'Girls!' he hissed.

Sure enough, there was the sound of distant female laughter. Rocky was on his feet, looking purposeful. Charles was up with him and they strode off together with Charles's phone playing island dancehall music like a mating call. Dilshan politely refused their invitation to join. He was deep in conversation with Alika.

'We'll bring you all back a girl. We're the hunters,' Rocky slurred. 'Even Coach has to have an island girl.'

Charles whooped his approval.

Joseph had been steadily chewing betel nut through the day and as he fixed his latest nut he offered me one. Micah roared gleefully. I turned to Dilshan, who just shrugged and grinned, and against my better judgement I accepted. I watched as Joseph cracked open a small nut, inserted a white powder and rolled it in a green leaf. He handed it to me.

'Chew in the corner of your mouth and don't swallow the juice. Spit it out.'

It tasted of burning. Every now and again I would feel the acrid red juices building up in my mouth and spit them out, but my mouth felt numb and I constantly felt like I needed to spit. After a day of various abuses, my body suddenly rebelled at the introduction of this latest invader. I tried to look calm and happy, but suddenly was certain I was going to be sick. I stumbled away from the group and spat the betel nut out. Slowly I started to feel human again and before long I was able to return to the others and grab another bottle of beer. It occurred to me that Joseph may have fixed the betel nut to be extra strong as a prank, but nonetheless it finally sank in just how damaging chewing betel nut every day must be. All the same, it had the effect I wanted and coaxed Joseph into finally talking to me.

'When you left the first time we didn't think you'd come back,' he said. 'Most of them don't.'

With that he stood up, swayed a little on his feet and strode off purposefully to urinate behind a hut.

Rocky and Charles returned and they weren't alone. The hunters had found their prey. They were being followed by a group of four young women, who were clearly just as drunk as them and struggling to stay on their feet. Nonetheless, I thought, the lads had done well for themselves. These were some of the prettiest girls I'd seen on the island.

'Hey, Dilshan, is that you?'

One of the girls bounced over to Dilshan and hugged him. It turned out they had been classmates at COM a couple of years back. Before long the other girls had followed their friend and were sitting in a circle around Dilshan. Rocky and Charles were aghast and stared at their captain with a mixture of respect and venom. They sat at the edge of the group, passing a bottle of rum between them and shaking their heads.

Eventually, Dilshan stood up and came over to Joseph and me. 'Let's go for a walk,' he said with a grin.

'See you in a bit,' he told the girls as Charles and Rocky pounced on their opportunity. Joseph and Micah slowly closed in on the group.

'I say we give them a couple of hours,' Dilshan laughed as we turned the corner to an altogether quieter part of the island to join the teetotallers Ryan and Roger.

The next day as we left Nahlap, I sensed a shift in my relationship with the team. Micah gave me a knowing nod and a smile as we climbed on to the launch. On the way back, Joseph and Rocky insisted that I sit in the back of the truck with them. When we went round a series of sharp corners, Charles leaned over and put his arm across me like a seat belt. In some small way I had become one of the locals. I had spent weeks trying to win the players' respect with my professionalism and made slow progress, but after one day of binge drinking I had won them over.

7

PROGRESS AND POLITICS

What had begun as a shower minutes before was now a deluge, a downpour of biblical proportions. The stream of water running off the roof of the stand sounded like a waterfall. Nonetheless, completely exposed to the elements that had already soaked them to the skin, a group of dedicated athletes was jogging round the running track at PICS Field. The only problem was that these weren't footballers; they were the island's track and field team. My players were nowhere to be seen. I was sitting in the stands, completely on my own.

While football had struggled to gain a foothold in Micronesia, athletics was an established, respected activity. Unlike our players, whose attendance was never guaranteed, the athletes turned up come rain or shine, or rain *and* shine, as was most often the case. Standing in the driving rain were the athletics coaches Michaela and George.

About the same age as me, Michaela had come to Pohnpei from America as a Peace Corps volunteer but had settled in and taken a job at the US embassy. She had begun coaching the track team in her free time and dedicated more and more of her time and effort to trying to get the best out of Pohnpei's young stars. I could hear her yelling orders through the driving rain. She sent her athletes off for a warm-up lap and came towards me, seemingly oblivious of the weather conditions.

'How are the soccer team getting on?' she asked.

I told her that things had been going well, but admitted that I had been left in the lurch. Not even Dilshan had turned up yet.

'It takes time for these guys to see you mean business,' she said sympathetically. 'At first they treated me terribly. It was even worse because I'm female. But if you just keep coming out here then eventually they realise you're not going to disappear and you really care.'

I asked Michaela for examples of what she'd had to put up with. She told me that on several occasions locals had followed her all the way home from PICS Field making lewd suggestions. While she'd be trying to teach athletes a technique, onlookers would stand around insulting her in Pohnpeian and telling her students not to listen to her. Michaela knew this because she'd learned the language very quickly and shocked the culprits by responding in their native tongue. After that, the insults stopped.

Michaela's colleague George, a jolly local, was making his way towards us and held out his hand with a smile. He added to Michaela's pep talk.

'Don't let things get to you,' he said. 'It's so hard to get sport taken seriously here. There's no funding for it, so people don't think they can get anywhere with it. I've been doing this for ten years and I end up spending my own money on equipment. The track is full of holes but what can we do? Just keep trying to make a difference because these guys do appreciate it, even if they don't always show it.'

Michaela and George returned to their hard-working athletes and left me to brood about the absence of mine. After the success of the trip to Nahlap I believed I was now accepted by the players. We'd had a very productive few weeks and even some I'd previously struggled to talk to had responded with enthusiasm to the drills. Micah was still giving me a smile and a raised eyebrow every time I asked him to do anything.

Now I felt let down and frustrated. The athletics team didn't have better facilities than we did. Their track was rotting and they had to deal with the same weather conditions, but they had one crucial advantage over us: the promise of competition. Micronesia has an Olympic Committee for a reason: to send athletes to the Olympics. Pohnpei's athletes knew that if they played their cards right they could end up on the biggest stage of them all. In the meantime they had the chance to travel to the nearby island of Palau for the Micro Games at the end of July. The Micronesian Games pits athletes from islands all over the Pacific against each other at a variety of sports including baseball, basketball, tennis, wrestling and even table tennis. Football wasn't chosen to be an event in Palau, largely because the host nation doesn't have a team.

Our footballers didn't have anything to aim for. When it was sunny and dry they would come to PICS because training was more fun than the precious few other leisure activities on offer. It wasn't like they had concerts, clubs or even TV to choose instead. But we needed the kind of dedication the track team had. We needed players to be obliged to turn up by some wider aspiration.

Items two and three on my Pohnpei checklist had been accomplished: we had built a league and selected a Pohnpei team from it. But how were we ever going to achieve the next aim of winning a game? As I sat in the stands my thoughts turned to Matt and how different things would have been with him in Pohnpei. In this exact same situation we would make light of it and let out our frustrations with a stream of jokes about the madness of our situation. Instead I was alone and thousands of miles away from my girlfriend and family, and all for what?

Eventually, Dilshan arrived with a carload of sheepish players he had rounded up after half an hour driving around Kolonia. I was seething and found it hard to hide my displeasure. I had spent a long time planning a session the whole squad could get something out of, and now all we had was six very late players and a sodden pitch. We practised a few crosses. I left them to play three on three and drove home having barely spoken a word. Dilshan could see that I wasn't happy. I knew I was taking things too personally, but it was hard not to. It was a long time since I'd had paid employment and any meagre savings I'd accumulated had long since evaporated. I had borrowed money from Lizzie, my parents and my brother and that had slowly disappeared too. I had been living on plain pasta for three weeks after blowing the last of my spending money on our trip to Nahlap. I'd lost a noticeable amount of weight and looked – and felt – like a ghost. Dilshan was in a similar situation. He had put off going to college so that he could concentrate on driving the growth of football, but without an education grant he was pretty much penniless. He lived at home with his parents but what he saved on accommodation he spent on petrol acting as family chauffeur. With his talent, Dilshan could have been in the US at college or in the Philippines playing semi-professionally. I could have been in London in a respectable job earning money and seeing friends. We'd sacrificed so much and yet our players couldn't even be bothered to turn up to training.

'We need someone to play and we need it soon. We've created a team but it won't work if there's nobody to challenge. People just turn up as and when they feel like it.'

I was at the Telecom Centre talking to Matt on Skype. He was in Los Angeles and around eighteen hours behind me. (Or was it ahead? We had given up trying to work out which.)

'The idea was always to get Pohnpei their first win,' he said. 'But it doesn't seem like anyone is playing in Yap or Chuuk. There wouldn't be much glory in turning up there and taking on eleven random people.'

'So I guess there's only one place we can really get to where there would be a team to play against,' I said as we both came to the same realisation.

'Guam.'

With the extortionate cost of flying in the region, the problem was obvious: how could we possibly afford to get a squad of Pohn-peians to Guam?

Some crude mathematics calculated a figure of £10,000 to get a sixteen-man squad to the neighbouring island.

'Don't worry about that right now,' Matt told me. 'I'll find us a sponsor. You just make sure we have a team.'

I found the Guam Football Association's website and sent an email to the general information address saying that a Pohnpei team would like to tour Guam. I chose not to call because I knew that any follow-up questions would be tough to answer on the spot.

Just before I logged off, an email arrived in my inbox. It was from FIFA's East Asian Football Federation, the department Tai Nicholas at the Oceania Football Confederation had told me to contact. I clicked excitedly.

RE: Football in Micronesia

Do not send any more unsolicited emails to this address.

Firstly, any email sent directly to me will be disregarded unless you approach through the correct channels. This is a gross error in protocol.

Secondly, all email communications must arrive from the secretary general of the Federated States of Micronesia Football Association along with evidence of his election and the by-laws of the organisation, so that a verification chain can begin.

We will disregard any further emails unless they meet these specifications.

That was all. I re-read the email over and over. There was no indication of who I should be emailing instead. Besides, I was pretty sure there was no such person as the secretary general of the Micronesia Football Association and I was almost certain there were no by-laws. It seemed that an island badly in need of help to develop football couldn't simply approach FIFA – they first had to jump through a series of patently unassailable hoops.

At the next training session, every one of the players had turned up at PICS. After talking to Matt I had driven round to Dilshan's house and told him our plan to conquer Guam. Although I took pains to stress how hard it would be to secure a sponsor, I could see the excitement on his face. He was ravenous for proper competition. Dilshan immediately started phoning round and told all the players we needed them to turn up for an urgent team meeting the next day at 4 p.m. And, amazingly, at 3.45 p.m. they were all there. I was still angry at the poor turnout the day before, but I had an ace up my sleeve and felt excited that I was about to use it.

'I've been disappointed that a few of you haven't been turning up to training,' I said, noting that most players were trying to avoid looking me in the eye. Rocky fixed a wild, menacing stare at Bob and Robert. Rodrigo, who was sitting next to his cousins, looked like he might cry.

'That's going to have to change. We're going to take a Pohnpei team to Guam and so we need everyone turning up to every session. If you're serious about football, then you must be here.'

The players didn't hear the last part because it was drowned out by the sound of excited whooping.

'But you've got to treat your coach with more respect,' Dilshan said. 'He's come all the way from England to teach us and you guys haven't been treating him right. No more messing around. You've got to be here, every time. And from now on, we're training five days a week.'

The speech had the desired effect. A shamefaced Bob came to apologise for his poor attendance record, blaming family pressures, but stressing that he would be more reliable. Charles, who had been absent for over a fortnight, happily told me that he had quit college again last week so he would have plenty of time for training. I almost believed them. The questions flooded in. When would we be going? Where would we be staying? How many games would we be playing? Can I bring my little son? I fended them off, trying to ignore the fact that I had more or less lied to the players. I had spoken as if the trip was a done deal but we had no real idea how we were going to fund it. It was a white lie told out of desperation because I was running out of money and patience.

The 'news' that we were going abroad spread like wildfire. Most of the players had never left the island, and immediately went home and told everyone who would listen that they were headed for Guam. The island rumour mill churned violently. Within hours of the announcement, Jim Tobin had called and told Dilshan and me to report to the Olympic Committee office the next day.

'So, you guys are going to Guam?'

Jim was ready to call my bluff.

'We're hoping to get some sponsorship. Matt's very confident that we will find a backer in LA or London,' I stuttered.

'Look, I really respect what you're trying to do, but it's very, very difficult to get sponsorship for a tour. People want their name on a building; they want something material. Local businesses may help but they don't have much money to offer and besides, they wouldn't trust that these guys would ever come back.'

I knew Jim was right. I tried to take the conversation in a sideways direction and told him how much improvement there had been in the players.

'You're doing a great job, but I know it's tough for you guys,' Jim said. 'You need funding. If I had my way you and Dilshan would both be on salaries.

'Next week the AGM of the Federated States of Micronesia Olympic Committee is being held in the conference hall at Yvonne's Hotel. The sports chiefs from all four islands will be there. If you can convince them that football is the sport to back then there's money to be had both from the International Olympic

Committee and from FIFA, but you'll have to persuade Clark Graham, the representative from Chuuk. He can be pretty volatile, to say the least.'

We had known for a long time that FIFA would only consider us for their £300,000 annual development bounty if we were a united FSM team with representatives from all four islands. The possibility of Olympic funding was enticing, but again required us to be Micronesia rather than Pohnpei. Attempting to create such a team would be fraught with political problems. All past meetings had ended in stalemate after heated arguments between the fiery Clark Graham and the Pohnpei representatives. If Dilshan and I had a lot of work to do on the pitch, we suddenly had just as much to do off it.

My efforts to engage FIFA had been an almost unqualified disaster. I later heard that Micronesia had been listed as a nation with 'no viability for football development' in a FIFA document three years earlier. There was no evidence that any FIFA delegate had been sent to the islands and the FSM was covered by just one line in a document spanning fifty-five pages. It read: 'Federated States of Micronesia: geographical difficulties, basic facilities present, no current activity, no review needed.' We had to get FIFA's attention, but I had been naïve in thinking I could do so without satisfying their endless appetite for eye-watering bureaucracy. We would need a formal Micronesian FA, we would need by-laws and committees and annual general meetings. We would need men in suits; men like Clark Graham.

'I know Clark pretty well,' Dilshan said as we left Jim Tobin's office. 'I lived in Chuuk for a few years and organised a high-school league there with him. If we can put on an exhibition game and impress him then he'll get really excited. He's one of those people who needs to see some proof it can work before he commits to anything.'

'Do you think we could get a decent Rest of the Island team together to play against Pohnpei State?' I wondered aloud.

'No, but I reckon we could get a good All Star XI from the best non-Pohnpeians in the Premier League,' said Dilshan.

Unlike most managers, I'd have to be responsible for picking the opposition team as well as my own. The Pohnpei Premier League had taught me that for every five players who promised to show, we would actually get three at best. We would need to invite at least twenty 'All Stars', which would mean lowering our standards somewhat. The name was starting to sound a little grander than the reality.

Steve Finnen would be able to bring several of his International FC players, while the rest would be the young Americans and Australians from the SDA side. I couldn't imagine anyone not wanting to take the chance to play against a newly formed national football team; what an amazing story to tell people when you get home. However, even after we explained the importance of the game to the SDA teachers they were reluctant to commit to turning up. A couple of them assured us that they would definitely be there as long as they were back from a surfing trip. The most enthusiastic SDA player was Brian Taylor, a goalkeeper of Marshallese descent, who had impressed us with his athletic saves during the Premier League.

The turnout for Pohnpei State team training still wasn't 100 per cent but it was certainly a lot closer. Already motivated by the prospect of a trip to Guam, the players were practically delirious with enthusiasm at the idea of taking on the Island All Stars.

'Time for Pohnpei to win!' Roger hollered.

'We're going to destroy the All Stars,' Ryan added.

Rocky stayed perfectly silent but a look of fierce determination spread across his face.

Having set the fixture and found the opponents, it was now absolutely essential that we won. I decided that there were two major weaknesses that needed to be addressed: a lack of positional awareness and, bizarrely, a reluctance to make physical challenges. In our first visit to Pohnpei we had been shocked by the brutality of some of the tackles, but since creating a State team the level of physical contact had steadily decreased and now training games were polite affairs with no crunching collisions. The players had become close friends and obviously felt nervous about injuring each other.

'I save the tackles for the proper games,' Robert explained one day after I reprimanded him for a particularly lethargic challenge on Dilshan. 'We shouldn't hurt each other, we should kill Guam.'

I tried to make the players see the importance of controlled aggression, even in training. I drafted a number of drills that encouraged contact and pitted two players against each other repeatedly, building a rivalry. Before we got started I explained that in Guam players wouldn't think twice about knocking them to the ground, so we needed to toughen up. Ryan looked worried, but my comments seemed to excite rather than daunt most of the squad. The change in mentality was immediately apparent. My first drill was a simple one: one player had to reach the ball but his opponent stood directly between him and it. I allowed the players to pair up against someone they thought they could outmuscle. The first two to go head to head were Ryan and Dilshan. I watched in astonishment as Ryan stood his ground. Dilshan finally pushed past him and his younger cousin flung out an elbow, catching

Dilshan in the chin. The players cheered wildly. Dilshan initially looked furious and for a second I thought he was going to lash out, but then he suddenly ruffled Ryan's hair. Time and time again players were sent crashing to earth, but they invariably returned to their feet with a smile. Bob and Robert paired up and produced an epic battle. Neither man reached the ball at all and the two had to be pulled apart before it became a fist fight. Despite being half their age, Rodrigo had again adopted the look of a put-upon parent.

Having five sessions a week gave me lots of time to work with the team. I took each player to one side and explained their position and what would be expected of them. We walked through match situations and ran defensive drills until everyone was thoroughly sick of them. Many of the exercises were simply designed to encourage the players to communicate on the pitch rather than playing in silence and waiting for Dilshan to tell them what to do; a legacy that had endured from the early days of the Pit Bulls when their captain taught them the basics. The incredibly slight Marvin was developing into a key player. His crosses were pinpoint and set up our aerial threat of Denson and Tom for header after header past the stranded goalkeeper. Strikers Ryan and Joseph were still reluctant to use their heads but Ryan was becoming a skilled poacher, finishing chances from ten yards out, while Joseph's right foot could unleash devastating strikes that belied his stature. One fizzing shot nearly fractured Alika's wrist as he attempted to save it.

The goalkeepers, Alika and Charles, were proving an odd pairing. Alika had taken on a semi-coaching role, to help iron out the bizarre quirks in Charles's game. While Alika had a natural technique, Charles was awkward and seemed to make everything as difficult as possible for himself. Instead of jumping in a controlled fashion to catch crosses as we taught him, Charles would invariably come flying through the air and land heavily on his head or neck, sometimes with the ball in hand, sometimes with the ball in the net. Meanwhile, Alika had done the drills we were doing before and was technically proficient, but his excess weight was very apparent and he ran out of steam while Charles was still warming up. At times both keepers were brilliant but neither of them looked entirely trustworthy. On the eve of the game against the All Stars we told the players they must arrive at PICS at 7 p.m. on the dot if they wanted to play. We then emailed Clark Graham an invitation to come and watch the game a few hours after his plane touched down in Pohnpei. All that remained to do was wait for my first official game as a coach.

As I arrived at PICS Field I was greeted by the heart-warming sight of thirteen excited players in various states of pre-match preparation. Wearing blue training shirts, to the untrained eye we could have been mistaken for a professional team, except for the shorts. As Matt and I had learned during our maiden kickabout all those months ago, the islanders' contempt for anything tight fitting meant that they rejected football shorts outright and opted for baggy versions in various styles.

Dilshan was already out on the field striking free kicks. I took a quick headcount. Thirteen. We were two short. I counted again and halfway through noticed we were missing the twins: Bob and Robert.

I looked for their cousin Rodrigo, who would surely have the answer to their whereabouts, and found him some way away from the other players very deliberately pulling on his socks and boots. As I approached, Rodrigo began to look nervous – not that I took that to be unusual. The baby-faced winger always looked terrified when anyone talked to him.

'Do you know where Bob and Robert are?' I asked.

'Sorry, Coach …' Rodrigo trailed off, muttering inaudibly and looking at the ground.

'It's OK, I'm not angry with you, but we need to know where they are.'

'They won't be here. They aren't allowed out yet.' Rodrigo was visibly shaking. I knew he was unable to disrespect anyone older than him, let alone an authority figure, but there was clearly something he didn't want me to know.

'They went to … to jail, Coach.'

'Jail?' I wasn't sure if something had been lost in translation.

'They were drunk and fighting, so the police took them to prison. They have to be there for one day.'

'Who were they fighting?' I asked.

'Each other. Their mother called the police. They told me not to tell you because they thought they might be able to get out. Please don't tell them I told you.'

I couldn't help but laugh. Rodrigo didn't seem to see the funny side. Once again he looked mortified. The news didn't really affect my team selection. In truth the twins, who were the oldest players on the team, had been the hardest to coach and were probably the least naturally talented. Bob had an infuriating tendency to put his head down and dribble the ball in a straight line, while Robert, perhaps too energised by my entreaties for more contact, was prone to making hideous and dangerous sliding tackles. I had tried to address both bad habits but with very little success. While younger players such as their cousin Rodrigo improved vastly from week to week, Robert and Bob were very much the same players we had met on our first scouting trip to Pohnpei. I found Dilshan giving Charles a pep talk and told him to lead the players in a warm-up; he looked more focused than I'd ever seen him before.

The line of blue shirts moved exactly in unison in complete silence. They looked like they meant business. Over the course of three months, a profound change had taken place in the players on a technical and also a mental level. They played like a team and thought like a team. It was crucial that we showed how far we had come with a resounding victory. I noticed with delight and anxiety that a reasonable crowd had gathered. Around thirty locals were intently watching the warm-up and occasionally one of them would call out something to one of the players, who would nod but not respond.

At the other end of the pitch were the 'All Stars', but I realised with a stab of panic that only five players had turned up on time. A couple of SDA volunteers were kicking a ball aimlessly across the boggiest part of the pitch, stopping to anxiously observe the Pohnpei State warm-up. They looked like they were thinking that this wasn't what they had signed up for. I looked at my watch. We simply had to find six more players to take on the State team or this whole publicity exercise would completely backfire. The visiting Chuuk official Clark would hardly give his backing to someone who couldn't even get twenty-two players on the pitch at the same time. Desperately scanning the crowd of spectators, I spotted Albert Carlot. Albert had come to Pohnpei from his native Vanuatu only eighteen months before to take a job with the Fisheries Commission and, like me, was still in the process of adapting to Micronesian life. Back in the French colony of Vanuatu, football ruled supreme and Albert was a regular for International FC despite a knee injury that prevented him from moving at anything like a sprinting pace. Albert's seventeen-year-old son, Matthew, was amongst the All Stars we had selected. Matthew looked a good couple of stone out of shape, but we weren't going to reject any willing volunteer.

'Any chance you fancy forming a father–son combo for the All Stars, Albert?' I asked, looking across at the outnumbered opposition.

'I was thinking you might need me to referee,' Albert grinned, producing a whistle.

In the frenzy of organising the teams, I had forgotten that one small detail.

'I'm a FIFA-qualified ref,' Albert added nonchalantly.

'What?'

'I passed the course fifteen years ago back in Vanuatu. The French FA helped the game a lot there and they provided a course. I'm not saying I'll be any good now!'

This was great news. Not only would I be able to focus on trying to coach the team without the complication of refereeing, the game would also surely benefit because, try as I might to be impartial, I would definitely have been biased. It would also give the game still more credibility to onlookers – especially the all-important Clark Graham. I had already decided that the Pohnpei substitutes would act as linesmen. We had trained them during the Pohnpei Premier League and they needed the experience. Under the watchful eye of a FIFA-qualified referee, what could go wrong?

Albert walked around the pitch, inspecting the lines I had marked out shakily, using cones and kicking at a few of the more obtrusive toads. I called the Pohnpei State players over before they could become distracted by the increasingly vocal supporters and gathered them around me. With Bob and Robert absent, the suspense surrounding my team selection diminished somewhat. Only one outfielder would have to be a substitute while the goalkeepers would take a half each. I gave young Rodrigo that undesirable role as Micah and Marvin took the starting positions on the wing. Typically timid, Rodrigo looked more relieved than disappointed not to be involved from the beginning.

I read out my team: Charles, Rocky, Tom, Denson, Roger, Nick, Dilshan, Micah, Marvin, Joseph and Ryan. After each name there was a cheer from the other players and occasionally a witty remark in Pohnpeian that was received with a hoot. I ran over the formation, more or less a simple 4–4–2, and reiterated the importance of short, sharp passing. I finished by telling them to have fun and left Dilshan to give them some final words of wisdom.

Things on the other side of the pitch didn't look so good. The 'All Stars' still only had ten men. I weighed up my options and realised I had only one: I would have to play against Pohnpei. It was something I had desperately wanted to avoid. I had planned for this to be my first game as a coach and had no intention of spending ninety minutes chasing my own players' shadows. We couldn't hold off any longer, though; the light would fade pretty soon and Albert was already making concerned gestures about how long we were taking to get ready.

'Paul, geezer!'

I turned, forgetting momentarily that I was in Micronesia rather than Hammersmith Broadway, to see Steve from Shepherd's Bush, the Englishman who had turned up briefly during a League match. Once again he had appeared from nowhere. Steve was wearing his customary Arsenal shirt and had turned up ready to play. He'd saved the day.

'Any room for a Tony Adams?' he smiled. 'I'll show these

Pohnpeians how to play the game. Then afterwards you and Dilly have to come round for a few beers.'

I happily accepted Steve's offer, gave Albert a thumbs-up and retired to the sideline, where Rodrigo was re-lacing the boots he had taken the best part of half an hour to lace the first time.

Albert gathered the captains together. Dilshan shook hands with All Stars skipper Mateus Barbosa, an Australian striker and SDA teacher who had been prolific in the Premier League. I felt a sudden pang of fear and powerlessness.

The whistle sounded.

'Let's go, Pohnpei!' a voice shouted from the sidelines. A few others were shouting in Pohnpeian.

Within five minutes we were 1–0 down. After all the training drills and tactical lessons, the goal was a freak event. A cross came over from the right, our goalkeeper Charles didn't come out to collect it so Roger had to blast it away, but his clearance rebounded off Matt Barbosa and into the corner of the net. It was the worst possible start. I tried not to panic and attempted to prevent my team doing so by shouting a stream of clichéd advice.

And then, at the worst possible time, Clark Graham announced himself. Having been told of his fearsome reputation, I was taken aback to see a small, meek-looking bald man in his forties with glasses. Apart from a tan that could only be earned from thirty years in the Micronesian sun, there was little to suggest that I was talking to Chuuk's sports chief.

Clark was very pleasant and softly spoken. He praised the pitch, the kits, the players and the sport of football, but admitted that he 'didn't have much idea of the rules'.

'I'm more of a basketball and wrestling man,' he said. 'But your guys look good, they're kicking it well.'

I tried to be polite, but I was incredibly distracted. We *were* now playing well, but the All Stars were holding their own. Marvin whipped in a devilish cross, but Shepherd's Bush Steve headed it clear, removing his glasses prior to contact and replacing them while yelling 'Eng-er-land!' in celebration.

The pitch looked better than ever before, but the bumps were playing havoc. Weeks of one-touch drills had encouraged our players to pass and move quickly, but bobbles were hampering our efforts to play flowing football. Dilshan beat four men and got a sight of goal but the ball stuck in a pothole, rolled backwards and squirmed away from him as he prepared to lash a shot.

I paced the sideline anxiously, growing more and more frustrated as promising attacks fizzled out again and again. The All Stars were playing hit-and-hope football, but they were defending effectively, like a non-league team trying to upset Premier League giants in the FA Cup. With every passing minute the intensity of the game increased.

Albert Carlot's son Matthew was acquitting himself well for the All Stars. He was clearly a good player, if lacking match fitness, and he would often show a deft touch but not quite be able to follow it up with a turn of pace. His right foot certainly had some power and I was relieved to see one effort skim the top of our bar.

Ten minutes before half-time, Roger picked up the ball in our box and found Marvin, who passed to Dilshan. Dilshan was running everything and he launched a long ball that evaded the All Stars defence and left Joseph Welson one-on-one with goalkeeper Brian Taylor. Joseph chipped it delicately. I held my breath. It clipped the underside of the bar and bounced into the net: 1–1. Joseph smiled briefly and then sulkily ignored the affectionate back slaps of his teammates.

At half-time I encouraged the players, who were despondent not to be ahead. I replaced Micah with Rodrigo and Charles with Alika and sent them back out. Charles threw his gloves on the floor and began to prepare his betel nut. After the break it was the same pattern. We attacked, they defended, the ball bounced around like crazy. Dilshan hit a free kick inches wide of the upright and then blasted a thunderbolt from twenty yards that the keeper flung himself dramatically to his right to save. Ryan was sent one-on-one but Brian saved at point-blank range. There seemed to be no way past the All Stars goalkeeper. Our fitness training was paying off, though, as the Pohnpei players seemed to grow in energy while the older All Stars flagged.

Clark was talking again.

'We should have something like this in Chuuk. It's fantastic for the youth. We have basketball and wrestling but soccer has never done as well. It's just that Pohnpei gets the funding and Chuuk never does.'

I didn't have the energy to discuss politics. I had become more vocal than I expected and was urging Rodrigo forward. The young winger was running his opposite number ragged but never called for the ball. Only Dilshan was talking on the pitch. The ball dropped to Joseph on the edge of the box; he paused and the All Stars defence regrouped, but just as the chance seemed to be gone, he produced a powerful, angled strike. Brian reacted with a full-length dive, but the shot was too powerful and he could only deflect it into the net. We were ahead, 2–1. Joseph nonchalantly walked back to the centre circle while the Pohnpeians in the stands cheered wildly.

The last few minutes were nervy. Suddenly the All Stars were pushing hard for the equaliser. What had started as a motley crew of coerced volunteers had become a motivated team, but Nick in midfield was breaking up attack after attack. Even more impressively, Nick was now barking orders at his teammates, acting as Dilshan's second-in-command. He'd only been playing football for a few months but he was already able and confident enough to direct players to their correct positions.

With seconds left, Matt Barbosa let fly from the edge of the box. My heart was in my mouth, but Alika dived low to his left and held on. Albert blew the final whistle. We had won.

Clark offered his congratulations and bid farewell. We'd be meeting him and the other sports leaders the next day. The players were elated. They were sitting in a circle joking and laughing. Roger danced while Joseph acted as a human beat-box.

I was torn. We had won and that was crucial, but in truth we had struggled past a team that included a few over-forties and several players who weren't even huge fans of football. There was a long way to go if we were to become a decent team, but I worried that it would be hard to prevent the players getting cocky.

My fears were unfounded.

'That was a horrible game,' Dilshan said as I approached.

'We played the worst ever, but we won,' Ryan agreed.

Speaking to the players, I felt reassured. None of them felt that they had played well but you could see their pride at having been involved in Pohnpei's first ever win.

'Today I am playing for my island and I love my island,' Nick said.

'I wouldn't want to live anywhere else in the world,' Marvin chipped in. 'Not even Guam.'

Joseph, the hero of the day, was much harder to read. I had run over to him and shaken his hand after the game, but he had seemed awkward and anxious to get away from me as soon as possible.

Now, after that brief spell of providing musical entertainment, while the rest of the players celebrated he slunk off down the road. He motioned at Charles to come with him, but Charles shook his head and stayed with the rest of his teammates.

That night Dilshan and I took Steve up on his offer and went over to his house for drinks. Steve lived in a guarded compound built by one of the richest families on the island. The houses in the compound are amongst the most expensive on Pohnpei, hence the rare desire for privacy and security. Steve answered the door with beers in hand and we were introduced to his wife, Emi, and his young son, who was wearing an England shirt. Steve had come to Pohnpei via the Marshall Islands, where he'd met his wife. Having lived in Shepherd's Bush for years, he had decided to get out and explore the world and had somehow ended up in the Pacific. In Pohnpei Steve did welding jobs to get by while his wife worked for a regional multi-governmental organisation.

'She's the brains in this operation,' he said.

Despite his self-effacing nature, it was clear that Steve was very intelligent and had managed to integrate into Marshallese and Pohnpeian society while still lapsing into cockney rhyming slang at the slightest provocation. Steve had become very sensitive to the Pohnpeian mentality and knew how to get things done. I learned that he had made the five-a-side goals for PICS Field and managed to get a wealthy Pohnpeian family to pay for them using some cunning island tactics.

'I had asked them for sponsorship and they said maybe, so I took another route. I went to Bill Jaynes at the *Kaselehlie Press* and told them that they had very kindly donated the goals. He ran the story and then they saw it and donated the money. They couldn't lose face, you see.'

As well as beers, Steve's wife had prepared a feast and Dilshan and I tucked into burgers, chicken, ribs and chips.

'I thought you needed feeding up,' Steve said. 'Someone's got to look after Capello and Gerrard.'

The Federated States of Micronesia Olympic Committee Annual General Meeting had entered its second hour. To my left was Jim Tobin, who looked weary. To my right were the Pohnpeian sports representatives for baseball, basketball, tennis and volleyball. Across the room sat Clark Graham from Chuuk, Paul Lane from Yap and Sterling Skilling from Kosrae.

'I think we should turn down our Olympic places,' the baseball representative, whose girth betrayed his lack of recent sporting activity, said. 'Then we could just keep the money for other things. We always lose so badly anyway.'

Jim didn't dignify that with an answer, changing tack instead.

'So, we're very excited that we have a blossoming soccer pro-gramme here on Pohnpei,' Jim declared with a nod in my direction.

'What's the point in soccer?' The portly baseball representative seemed to be on a mission to antagonise Jim. 'I mean, whoever heard of a Pohnpeian playing soccer?'

'Actually we've had more participation in soccer than baseball this year and baseball is getting ten times more funding. Maybe you should go up to PICS Field one night this week,' Jim growled.

'I'll be watching the baseball in the evenings.'

Frustrated by the pace of the meeting, Jim announced that anyone interested in Micronesian football should leave the room to meet next door. I got up and left and was pleased to see the representatives from the other islands join me. Our 'meeting room' was the refreshment room with a table of plates stacked with the most fattening of pastries, doughnuts and a few dangerous-looking sandwiches. Seconds after I'd sat down the door opened again to admit Dilshan, arriving just in time after driving his mum to work in Palikir. Chewing gum, as ever, he shuffled up to Clark and the two affectionately shook hands.

While Dilshan and Clark reminisced about old times, Yap's representative Paul Lane introduced himself. Paul was American born and hadn't been in the region that long, but like Jim and Clark he was on track to becoming Micronesian. Yap is a much more traditional island than Pohnpei and embracing the Yapese lifestyle meant taking part in local spear-fishing events, carefully winning the acceptance of tribal leaders and becoming used to the sight of topless women, as is the custom. Paul Lane had the deeply contented look of a man who had found a loophole in life. He worked four-hour days and spent the afternoons on the ocean in his boat with a cooler of beers, but was still regarded as working harder than the locals thought necessary.

'Yap used to be the home of soccer in Micronesia and I want to get the game going again,' he said. 'I think it's a much more suitable sport for locals than basketball, which receives almost all our funding. We were paying ridiculous amounts of money to people just to sit on the scoring table. I cut that as my first act on Yap and, I can tell you, some people wanted to kill me!'

Since the glory days at the start of the twenty-first century, football in Yap had faded and been largely forgotten. The Yap Sports Complex still had the best facilities in the Federated States of Micronesia and Paul told us there was a pristine football pitch lying unused that would put PICS Field to shame. However, the lack of anyone to coach football was proving an insurmountable obstacle while basketball flourished. The only true Micronesian native in the room was Sterling Skilling, the sports chief from the sleepy island of Kosrae, best known as a divers' paradise. He was an amiable middle-aged man wearing the customary Hawaiian shirt.

'There's never been soccer in Kosrae, but I would like to try and bring it in because I think it would be good for our young people,' he said softly. 'They love canoeing and spear fishing but there just isn't enough for them to do.'

Sterling told us that he had heard about our progress in Pohnpei, not from the local grapevine but from a stream of emails from European football fanatics asking about the possibility of a coaching job in the same mould as mine.

'These gentlemen seemed to think we would be able to pay for them to come out to coach soccer. I didn't want to be rude so I didn't reply,' Sterling said with a shrug.

Clark spoke up. 'Seeing as I am the secretary general of the Federated States of Micronesia Football Association, I think I should lead proceedings.'

I looked at Dilshan and he shrugged. This was news to him as well. Clark Graham was the mysterious secretary general of Micronesian football that FIFA had demanded contact them.

'I saw Pohnpei's team play a match yesterday and was very impressed. This is something I want in Chuuk and I'm sure Paul and Sterling feel the same for their islands.

'But we need to end this pro-Pohnpei bias. Everything happens on Pohnpei because it's the rich American island and on Chuuk we get forgotten about. We need Paul and Dilshan to visit all the islands, not to stay on one.'

'We'd be happy to have them,' Paul Lane said, and then addressed Dilshan and me directly. 'We have good funding and facilities in Yap, and topless women!'

The meeting continued amicably, but Clark was determined to stress the importance of making a national programme, rather than a Pohnpei programme. At one point he lapsed into a lengthy tirade against the imbalance in health funding between Chuuk and Pohnpei and political prejudices. Clark had tried to approach the East Asian Football Association to seek FIFA membership a decade ago, but he claimed that Pohnpei had been the weak link on that occasion and stalled proceedings. This time, he insisted, it would need to be a joint effort.

An hour later, we were in agreement. Clark would remain secretary general of the Micronesia Football Association and would be in charge of the paperwork. International FC captain Steve Finnen would officially be the president. We hoped that a respected and well-spoken lawyer would give us added validity in the eyes of FIFA. Dilshan would be vice-president, charged with the hands-on development of the game. Paul Lane would help him when he was in Yap while Sterling would find someone to help him on Kosrae. I would be the national coach. Despite my excitement at the idea of being the man to create a united Micronesian national team, I could see that it would be easier said than done. Clark was going to pursue FIFA funding, but until we had that there was no way I could afford to visit Yap, Chuuk or Kosrae, let alone buy the necessary equipment. We barely had enough for Pohnpei.

For the moment, the new role wouldn't change anything. The tour of Guam was a Pohnpei tour – we were planning to leave within three months and it would be farcical, as well as unfair to our players, to pick a representative from each of the other islands to be integrated for simply political reasons. The sixteen best players in Micronesia at the moment were on Pohnpei, but to label a completely Pohnpeian team 'Micronesia' would surely cause political chaos. A true national team would have to wait until we received some funding, and impressing on our tour would be the best way to show we were a worthy investment.

Dilshan picked up the ball and squared it to Marvin, who flicked it on to Ryan. Putting his body between the ball and Denson's boot, Ryan chested the ball back to Joseph, who instinctively unleashed a rocket of a shot that was set to rip the goal net off until Rocky came flying at full stretch to head clear. We were starting to look like a football team. It hadn't been a miraculous transition but rather the result of endless arduous practice. We spent hours playing one-touch games, dribbling round cones and perfecting set-piece moves. I was shocked to find myself tiring of the drills before the players did. The greatest improvements came from the hardest workers. Rocky had become an uncompromising defender with an impressive eye for the game. Nick looked every bit a defensive midfielder while Ryan was finally beginning to embrace the physical side of the game. He'd also learned to drive and developed a bit of a swagger, partly due to his new female fan base of fellow SDA pupils who often turned up to cheer him on. The other players found it hilarious, but Ryan didn't seem to mind their jokes.

Dilshan continued to work himself into the ground and took Rodrigo and Marvin under his wing. Shy Rodrigo improved noticeably under his direction but the process of injecting fight into the meek midfielder seemed to exasperate Dilshan, who couldn't understand anyone not playing every game as if his life depended on it.

I was trying to create a team that I felt could win football matches, but I knew how important it was that I was creating a Pohnpei team, not an English team in Pohnpei. I knew not only that I couldn't take Micronesia out of the players but that I shouldn't.

I had always been coached in a very traditional English style and I could see both its benefits and drawbacks. When teaching basic techniques and tactics it had helped to use a traditional set of rules, but now that players were learning to express themselves on the pitch, I had to find a way to guide them rather than indoctrinate them in the ways of 4–4–2 English football. Every now and again I would see a defender get the ball in a dangerous position with two strikers bearing down on him and be staggered as he attempted to pick his way past them with deft footwork. Sometimes it would work and his team would launch a brilliant counter-attack. Sometimes it wouldn't and he would concede a goal. But his teammates would never yell at him to get rid of the ball under pressure or ever moan at him for giving away a goal when things went wrong. There simply wasn't that fear or frustration that underlies British football and shaped my growth as a footballer. Any English lad playing in defence is told that, when in any doubt, he should hoof the ball as far away as possible, even if that means sending it off the pitch, over the stand and into the river. Safety always comes first. And so, whenever the situation arises, his teammates and coach will yell at him to do exactly that. That instinct always remains with you regardless of whether you're playing for East Fulham or Manchester United. I knew that I had to introduce the concept of sensible defending without crushing the players' unique freedom.

Bob and Robert were as unreliable as ever, but I suspected that they would only ever play bit parts in the team. The more worrying absence was that of Alika, who had suddenly stopped coming to training entirely. Dilshan, who knew Alika well, told me that he was looking after his gravely ill mother. Alika's father had left the island five years ago and Alika had taken the role of man of the house very seriously.

One afternoon before training, Dilshan came to my hotel room and laid a copy of the *Kaselehlie Press* in front of me.

'FSM's former first lady passes away,' read the main headline.

I tried to work out exactly what Dilshan wanted me to say. I scanned down the article and stopped at the line 'Lady Iris Falcam served as the First Lady of the Federated States of Micronesia during the tenure of the great president Leo Falcam from 1999 to 2003.' Falcam was Alika's surname.

'Did you know that Alika's dad was the president?' I asked in shock.

'Of course,' Dilshan said. 'Everyone knows, but he doesn't like to make a big deal of it. It just helps when you get pulled over by police or get any trouble on a night out.'

I remembered that day out to Nahlap and how Alika had dealt with the police officer.

'How is he?'

'He's not good. I don't think he'll be playing football again for a while. It could be weeks or it could be months, but it's going to be the last thing on his mind.'

The prospect of having to rely on Charles as our only goal-keeper was scary. When he turned up and tried he was a great keeper, but so often he would fail to arrive or play lethargically, making a string of basic mistakes. Dilshan and I didn't even have to discuss our options: we immediately called Brian Taylor, the SDA teacher who had thwarted us on so many occasions for the Island All Stars, and told him he was in. Brian was a strange presence at training. Having been born in the Marshall Islands and raised in California, he was not Pohnpeian in any sense, but principles could only go so far; we needed a second goalkeeper, not least to convince Charles he still needed to come to training. If he thought he had a guaranteed place in Guam we wouldn't see him again until it was time to board the plane. While Brian wasn't Pohnpeian, one of the few benefits of FIFA's failing to recognise Pohnpei was that selection for the Pohnpei State team was bound only by the same rules as any other club side: we could pick more or less anyone we liked.

Of course, I could have picked myself – that had initially been the whole point of the exercise, after all – but being an international footballer no longer seemed quite so important.

The new man stood out like a sore thumb. Brian was a fantastic athlete, thinking nothing of flying acrobatically to make a diving save, but his slightly camp Californian accent and reluctance to come out for any one-on-one made the rest of the team, and especially Rocky, suspicious of him. I worked closely with Brian and found him an enigma. On one hand he happily told me that he 'didn't really like soccer, not as much as American football', then he would turn up half an hour early to training to get extra practice at claiming corners. Brian was proof of how fickle the football gods can be: he may not have had any great passion for the game, but he had been blessed with a lot of natural talent. We looked a lot safer at the back with him around.

I knew there was something Lizzie wasn't telling me.

I was perched on a bench outside the Telecom Centre, talking into my laptop while trying to ignore a local boy no older than ten who was spitting betel-nut juice into a can placed a few feet in front of him – a party trick it must have taken most of his young life to master.

The internet connection was on typically poor form. As ever, I had been forced to redial four times in a twenty-minute conversation and, as ever, FSM Telecom had seen fit to charge me $20 for those frustrating minutes online. I had spoken to Lizzie every day since I'd arrived in Pohnpei and we'd generally kept conversations upbeat, focusing on planning for the future rather than dwelling on the fact that we were separated by a great deal of the planet's land and sea. But over the last week or so our chats had been much shorter and she had sounded sad, lacking her usual energy.

'Promise me you won't worry,' she said.

I braced myself for an explanation.

'I've got swine flu. I haven't been able to get out of bed for a week. I can't eat, drink or even sleep.'

I promised to be on the next flight home, which was two days away. As we spoke, I began looking for flight times.

'That's why I didn't tell you,' Lizzie said. 'I don't want you to rush home because what you're doing is so important. You'll be back in three weeks anyway, and I'll be OK until then.'

I trawled the internet for information on swine flu, hoping to see something that reassured me. The first headlines invited panic. 'UK Swine Flu Deaths Reach Twenty-Nine'; 'Global Pandemic Fears as Swine Flu Deaths Rise'.

The information I could find was full of mixed messages; some sites stressed that swine flu was no more dangerous than ordinary flu to a healthy person while others told of perfectly healthy adults dying from it. Lizzie was adamant that she was steadily getting better, but even on the typically grainy line she sounded worn out.

Despite my promise to return home immediately, I knew it probably wasn't possible. There were so few planes flying with so few seats that the next available flight was a fortnight away, just five days before I was booked to go back anyway, and to change my travel dates would cost $150 that I simply didn't have. There was nothing much I could do. As I sat panicking, two emails arrived in my inbox almost simultaneously: one from the Guam Football Association and one from my mum.

I opened my mum's first.

From: Margaret Watson
Subject: Are you OK?

Hi Paul,
I've just seen on the news that Pohnpei is on a tsunami warning. Can you let us know that you are OK as we're a bit worried?

I had heard about the tsunami warning the day before while on the internet and called Dilshan in a panic. He'd laughed calmly and told me that Pohnpei was nine miles inland from the reef. There really was nothing to worry about. The locals certainly weren't concerned. Nobody had any idea that the island was on red alert. There were no signs, no announcements and, slightly worryingly, no evacuation plans in the event of a tsunami hitting. I dropped the tsunami warning into conversation with a petrol station attendant and asked him what he would do if it hit Pohnpei.

He seemed to think hard for a while and then said: 'Swim.'

I sent my mum a suitably calm reply, letting her know that no natural disaster had ever hit Pohnpei.

Then I excitedly opened the reply from the Guam Football Association that had been written by a man called Tino San Gil, who introduced himself as the secretary general of the FA.

Dear Paul,

Thank you for your email. We are very excited to hear that football is up and running in Pohnpei once more. Any Pohnpei team would be very welcome here for a tour. Are you planning on coming to Guam anytime soon? We could organise to show you around and make some plans.

Best wishes

Tino San Gil

I would be heading home via Guam in three weeks' time. My current itinerary had me there for six hours – a typically lengthy waiting period before boarding a flight to Seoul, where I would connect to London.

The waiting times on the journey were torturous. While businessmen would be put up in hotels and break the travelling up into three, my tight budget forced me to spend four hours on the floor of the departures lounge in Manila in a semi-catatonic state clutching my bag for dear life. In normal circumstances I would have tried to change my flights to grab two or three days in Guam, but I had spent five months without my girlfriend and now I knew she was ill. I wanted to get back to London as quickly as possible and even seventy-two extra hours en route was too long. I decided I would have to meet Tino and do a whistle-stop tour of Guam before getting back on a plane and continuing the journey. I told

Tino I would be in Guam sooner than he could possibly have expected.

The next three weeks were a challenge. In truth I was counting down the days until I could get home. I tried to hide my distracted state of mind from the players, but I didn't do a great job. I confided in Dilshan, he told Charles and before long it became the squad's worst-kept secret that my girlfriend wasn't well. Touchingly, the players seemed to work harder and began to police themselves. For the main part it was Dilshan who took the burden of responsibility, but when Charles turned up forty minutes late he was told off by Rocky and when Bob began to mess around during a possession drill it was Denson who intervened with some terse Pohnpeian.

Two days before my departure I returned from my morning jog to find a parcel on the bed. I immediately recognised the writing as Lizzie's but was taken aback by the state of the package, which looked as if it had been attached to the back of a mail van and dragged from London to Pohnpei. Lizzie had sent a care package just after I'd left London months before, filled with things she thought I'd miss in Micronesia. An overconfident post office clerk in Chiswick had bullishly assured her that it would be delivered 'within five to seven working days' – an impressive boast, given that it can take a week to get a letter to Essex. Three weeks later Lizzie had received an apologetic phone call explaining that the parcel had been sent to Macedonia rather than Micronesia. Incredibly, though, it did finally arrive. The books and magazines were dog-eared, a box of tea bags had been opened and a Cadbury's Creme Egg had been reduced to its constituent molecules, but, amazingly, the Bourbon biscuits had survived intact. It had arrived just in time for me to leave.

I needed to get back to England to look for sponsors to make a tour of Guam a genuine possibility. I needed to finally get hold of the shirts Matt and I had designed. But most of all I needed to see Lizzie and make sure she was OK. At the airport I paced around excitedly. For the last two weeks Lizzie and I had been talking of nothing but what we would do when I returned to England. Finally, the time had arrived.

'Look at this guy,' Charles said, snorting with laughter. 'He really misses his girlfriend!'

Rocky smiled.

'Enjoy civilisation,' Dilshan said as we hugged goodbye at the airport. I realised that I'd miss him.

I reflected on my second spell in Pohnpei. It had been months of getting bitten by mosquitoes and chased by dogs, of missing my girlfriend and my family. But I had also fallen for Pohnpei and come to see Dilshan as my brother on the island. In those few months I'd managed to be simultaneously happier and sadder than at any other point in my life.

I had been to Guam's Antonio B. Won Pat airport on several occasions en route to Pohnpci, but this time I was going to visit Guam proper.

Seen as the Las Vegas of the Central Pacific, Guam is a US territory and landing on the island is administratively just like arriving in New York. The significance of Guam to the US doesn't take long to announce itself. 'God Bless Our Troops,' a huge sign declares as you leave the airport. Guam is an army base and a strategic outpost, allowing the US to better protect Hawaii. The metropolis of

Hagåtña has developed as an extension of the army base that covers most of the north of the island. It's a grid of dual carriageways lined with fast-food restaurants, bars and endless strip clubs – the latter may explain why Guam has the world's highest rate of divorce. The island has five times the population of Pohnpei and, to Pohnpeians, Guam is nirvana: it's the USA without leaving Micronesia.

Tino had come to meet me and greeted me warmly before leading me to his car, which had the Guam Football Association logo on the back of it. He explained that it had been donated by sponsors. I was entering an alternative footballing reality.

After months on sleepy Pohnpei, the car seemed to be going at 100 mph as we drove to the Guam Football Complex, but Tino put me at ease with his laid-back attitude and sense of humour.

'The last time I was on Pohnpei, the only football I saw was three guys kicking a ball on PICS Field,' he said. 'That pitch is pretty terrible, eh? It reminded me of how we used to be until we got FIFA funding.'

We turned off the main road and into the GFA complex. On the main pitch, which was pristinely marked and cut, two teams of eleven-year-olds were playing in front of a crowd of at least fifty eager parents.

'On weekends we have games all day from 9 a.m. to 9 p.m.,' Tino said proudly. 'We get around ten thousand people down here during the course of a week.'

Tino conducted a tour of the facility that FIFA built for Guam's Football Association. In addition to two beautiful full-size pitches there were mini-pitches of all sizes and even a beach football pitch filled with imported sand. We sat down in one of the plush offices and Tino listened enthusiastically while I outlined our progress over the last few months.

'Our president, Richard Lai, took over when we had one terrible pitch and a handful of players. Now we have thousands of players of all ages,' Tino said when I finished.

Despite being a US territory, Guam is treated by FIFA as an independent nation and receives the annual development budget of between £150,000 and £400,000 that is given to all member nations. This funding is the culmination of a lengthy process that involves joining your regional football federation (in this case East Asia) and spending smaller development grants to FIFA's satisfaction for three years. Each step requires a mountain of paperwork. The more participation in football FIFA see, the more money a nation is eligible for.

'To get any money we needed to have committees for each facet of the game,' Tino explained. 'We also needed strong paper proposals and a wealth of local sponsors. It was tough here but we do have big US companies on the island, it must be even harder on Pohnpei.'

I spoke confidently about getting a sponsor in the US or the UK to fund a tour to Guam, feeling like a fraud as I did so.

'I think it would be a huge step for Micronesian football if you could get a team here,' Tino said. 'We would assist in any way we could to try and keep costs down once you were here. If people see Pohnpei playing and they look good then it will show some important people that Micronesia deserves funding.

'We're pretty booked up here in Guam but we have one week free at the start of October. It'll have to be that first week of October if a Pohnpei team is going to come over this year.'

I believed that Tino would help us if we could get to Guam, but I suspected that he didn't quite expect us to make it. Going on the word of one twenty-six-year-old sunburned Englishman, why should he? I left for home feeling dispirited rather than encouraged. Guam was clearly ascending the football hierarchy and was one of FIFA's success stories. However, while it was a model to aspire to and proof that football can thrive in the Pacific, I was concerned by the number of ways we were different from them. Somehow we would have to find willing and able locals to chair committees, wade through laborious paperwork and write persuasive letters to FIFA, all on a voluntary basis for the time being. We'd had enough trouble getting twenty-two players to turn up to a league match on time.

Guam had started with nothing, but Tino told me that Richard Lai, their FA president, was an extremely influential Asian businessman with a wealth of contacts within FIFA. We didn't have Guam's contacts, we didn't have their money men and we couldn't call on the US for help. The annual Compact Agreement payment made by the US to Micronesia doesn't include anything for sport, let alone football, a sport America hardly regards as a priority. The only way we could conceivably get a foot on the football ladder was with a leg-up from our big brother, Guam. We just had to show Tino and his president that football in Micronesia was worth a gamble and that they should vouch for us. Getting a team to Guam would be enough of a task, but I realised that we'd have to do more than just turn up if we were to make a lasting impact. We'd need to win.

8

THEIR COUNTRY NEEDS YOU!

I felt disoriented, and not just because I was on a train to Yeovil. The reality of returning to England hadn't been quite what I had expected. It was just fantastic to see Lizzie. After the initial shock of being in the same place after so long, we revelled in being able to chat any time without fighting a grainy phone line and dizzying time difference. However, the feeling that things weren't quite right started to build: Lizzie was firmly on the road to recovery, but she still wasn't entirely herself – it was clear she had been very ill – while my financial situation was dire. Simply put, I had no money and Lizzie had no energy.

London suddenly seemed an alien environment. Minutes after I returned to Heathrow I had seen a man knock a woman over in a fight for a luggage trolley. Cars seemed to hurtle past at Formula 1 speeds, dogs were attached to leads and there were people *everywhere*. Out of habit I greeted a stranger on the street with a nod; he looked at me with a mixture of fear and disgust. While I always felt like a Londoner on Pohnpei, now I suddenly felt like an islander in London. In Pohnpei I had spoken confidently about getting sponsorship and made plans to approach the

English Football Association for a grant to do my coaching badges. Naturally, sponsorship for Pohnpei State was the priority: without it I wouldn't even be able to return to the island, let alone take a team to Guam. I was like a gambler on a losing run. I was down, but I knew that if I gave up on Pohnpei now all the money I'd spent so far would be wasted – not to mention the huge investment of time and energy – and there would be nothing to show for it, but to get any further I'd have to plough in still more money that I didn't have.

Getting some coaching qualifications was important as it would give us a greater legitimacy in the eyes of FIFA – the organisation we were ultimately looking to impress. Besides, if I could learn how to coach properly then I would be better placed to pass that knowledge on to our players, who would be the coaches of tomorrow in the region. Somehow I had managed to forget how hard it had been to raise any interest in supporting Pohnpei when we were looking for kit and sponsorship. It began to dawn on me exactly how difficult it would be to achieve my targets when an email from the FA arrived, responding to my request for a discount on a coaching course. I planned to use the qualification to further football in Micronesia: a goal exactly in line with FIFA's mission statement. I opened the email and wasn't at all surprised by the response.

Thank you for your email, but I am afraid we cannot help with individual funding.

I barely had enough money to get by on a day-to-day basis, so the coaching qualifications would have to wait. I turned to my Plan B. I was in regular contact with Chris Sweet, a journalist who worked for the *Western Gazette* covering various football teams in Somerset and Dorset. He was fascinated by the Pohnpei story and had arranged for Toolstation League Premier Division side Sherborne Town to donate some shirts, socks and shorts that had been SDA FC's kit for the first Pohnpei Premier League season. In return I'd written some pieces for the Sherborne Town match programme and a strange bond had been forged.

I knew that Chris did a lot of his work at Yeovil Town, who were a League One side, and on returning to England had asked whether it would be possible for me to watch Yeovil train. Unexpectedly the Yeovil manager, Terry Skiverton, had given the thumbs-up. I figured that I could learn more from watching a professional team train than I could on any coaching course, so I headed for Yeovil Junction. One of the youngest coaches in the Football League, Terry Skiverton had switched from player to manager at Yeovil at the tender age of thirty-four. Despite the slight difference in our football career paths – Terry having made over 400 appearances as a professional player – I hoped that on some level he might understand my plight, trying to be taken seriously as a young coach. With the end of the season approaching and a relegation battle coming to its climax, Terry had more pressing matters to attend to than giving me a coaching master class, but it was interesting to see his methods. Everything was much quicker, smoother and more polished than our drills on PICS Field but I was heartened to see that a professional training session wasn't entirely unrecognisable from one of my own devising. I had time to ask Terry one question: how can I make my players more aggressive in training?

'You've got to make things personal,' he said. 'Have two players competing throughout a session and let them pick out who they take on. If it's a matter of pride then they'll show the same intensity as in a match.'

I returned home to find we had received some further donations. Some were from people who had seen Pohnpei in the press; most were from members of Lizzie's family. Lizzie's relatives always championed my cause and their contributions alone had allowed me to buy boots for the entire squad. But generous as these donations were, they would never be enough to get us to Guam.

A commercial sponsor was proving harder to find. A chicken-feed company in Cumbria sent an email out of the blue and flirted with putting their name on our shirts, but they refused to pay more than £2,000 for that privilege. Even that modest offer was retracted when the head of the company had second thoughts about whether publicity in Micronesia would help him conquer the lucrative Penrith pullet-pellet market. Having been rejected by a chicken-feed company, I felt I was running out of options. It was time to play my ace card, even though I had been determined to do so only as a last resort. I called my brother, Mark. The whole Pohnpei idea owed a lot to our shared childhood obsession with obscure footballing nations and during the build-up to my first departure for Micronesia I discussed my plans at length with him. We were in weekly contact when I was in Pohnpei, partly because of a football prediction game that we competed in. For the last four years Mark and I had bet on twenty football games every week, battling to see who could forecast more correct results. Every Friday without fail we send each other our bets and my being on the other side of the world didn't change that, even if I'd eventually given up on staying awake until 5 a.m. every Saturday to see how many I'd got right. Mark is a successful stand-up comedian and, having heard all about our current financial predicament, he had mentioned that he might be able to host a comedy fundraising event in London. It was a nice offer but one that I hadn't intended to take advantage of, partly because I didn't want to add to his busy schedule and partly because I didn't want a label on my work in Pohnpei that included the phrase 'comedy project'. I had learned my lesson from our first foray into the world of media. However, at this stage, with no sign of a sponsor on the horizon, beggars couldn't be choosers.

Mark went about calling in favours and setting up an evening of stand-up that centred on an eBay auction of various signed items, as well as some Pohnpei-related lots. The evening was titled 'Mark Watson's Football Shambles'. It was an apt description. With just days remaining before the show, the venue was booked – the 400-seat Leicester Square Theatre – but every other area of the show remained nebulous. As we couldn't afford to pay anyone, all the guest acts were 'probably coming'. Mark was busy with other projects right up until the day and had very little time to focus on writing anything, so there was no running order either.

On the other side of the Atlantic, after almost a year spent on the sidelines, Matt took the brave (some might say rash) decision to fly back for the fundraiser. His course at USC had just ended and he landed a matter of hours before the show was scheduled to start, looking jet-lagged and making very little sense. We barely had time to say hello to each other before we were on stage with Mark.

The evening proved a success in terms of entertainment. Almost all the guests who had promised to come were true to their word and there was even a cameo appearance from football anchor Jim Rosenthal, who was in the audience. Despite turning up with no plan at all, Mark held the rest of the evening together impressively. The eBay auction provided some unexpected revenue: we couldn't hide our amazement as an anonymous bidder offered nearly £30 for a Burnley FC rubber duck Mark had been given on the Sky Sports show *Soccer AM*. Tickets to Mark's show and signed copies of his books raised much larger sums and things were looking up. I went home with a collection bucket that had been passed round at the end of the evening and excitedly looked forward to counting our windfall. The eBay lots had raised nearly £700. The collection came in at just over £80, much of which was in 2p pieces. Ticket sales had been cancelled out by the cost of hiring the venue, so the grand total from the evening was £781.34, leaving us short of our Guam target by just £9,218.66.

As the extent of our failure sunk in, an email arrived from Dilshan, heartbreakingly full of optimism.

Hope all is well in England and that things are looking good for sponsorship. The guys here are training really hard because everyone wants to get a place in Guam. Since you left we've been doing long runs every morning to make sure we're in shape so that when you come back we can get to work.

I wanted to ask whether it would be OK for Matthew Carlot to train with us? He's lost so much weight, nearly 15kg, and is desperate to get a place in the team. He's a good striker and is getting better from playing against us. You must remember when he played for the All Stars against us and how good he was.

Tom Mawi hasn't been around because he has been selected to go to the Micronesian Games with Pohnpei's basketball team. He seemed upset because he knows he probably won't get to go to Guam, but he had no choice really. He said that as soon as he returns he'll come back to training even if he can't play for the team – he should be back by the time you get here.

We're doing our best to help raise money by doing car washes. We were under the sun for 6 hours yesterday at Palm Terrace. The whole team was there and we raised nearly $200.

See you soon.

Dilshan

Matt and I couldn't think how to reply. The thought of the players washing cars all day believing they would be going to Guam was horrific. The guilt was awful. We had asked Continental to hold the seats we needed to Guam while we 'finalised' our sponsorship. They told us that the money must be transferred by the end of June or the tickets would be put on general sale. The chances of eighteen seats remaining unsold on a generally busy flight were slim to nil.

The World Cup had begun in South Africa. Four years ago in Italy we had lapped up every game with endless enthusiasm. Now we could hardly find the energy to watch any. As England meandered to their routine exit in the knockout stages and the nation's media reacted to a heavy defeat against Germany as if lives had been lost, even I was surprised at how little I cared. We had a matter of days to prevent our own footballing disaster and find a last-gasp sponsor.

It was the 29th of June. We had two days left before Continental cancelled our flights to Guam. Spain were playing Portugal in the last sixteen. It was a terrible game. A scrolling billboard in the background read: 'FIFA: Touch the world, build a better future'. I felt the bile rise in my throat. Matt and I would occasionally glance at the screen to see whether Spain had scored their inevitable winner yet, but we were focused on our alternative football reality. We were holding crisis talks. Dilshan had told us in another email that some of the players were starting to ask questions about the arrangements for Guam and how certain it was we would be going. He'd been put in an awkward position and was starting to realise that he ran the risk of being labelled a false prophet. He had to believe in us, but must have been starting to wonder if he had been right to do so.

Matt and I were sitting in exactly the positions we had been in when the Pohnpei idea was born, but now we were both totally jaded. There wasn't a hint of the good-natured grandstanding that had inspired the project in the first place. On the table was a list of nearly a hundred potential sponsors, ranging from the overly ambitious (Adidas and Nike) to the last resort (Spam). Over half the names had been crossed out; the others were marked 'no response'.

'I'm going to call Larry again,' Matt said.

'Larry?'

'Larry Coyne, Coyne Airways. They're third from bottom in the eighth row.'

Larry Coyne was a close friend of Matt's family. He had set up an air-cargo business and made a name for it by flying to countries other airlines wouldn't go near. Larry had known Matt since he was born and was a regular visitor in the Conrad household. The call was answered and Matt put it on speakerphone, so I could hear Larry's Irish tones.

'Mazza, I was just about to call you,' Larry said. 'In your email you said that you needed ten thousand pounds, is that right?'

'Well, ten thousand is the full total but we could be looking for two sponsors for less. I know it's a lot at the moment,' Matt replied.

'I'm in,' Larry said simply. 'We'll get you the ten thousand. If you can get some shirts made with Coyne Airways as the sponsor then it's a deal, and if you can get me an international cap, then I'll double it!'

I still can't remember the rest of the conversation as the logistics of the deal seemed pretty irrelevant. I had stopped believing we'd find a sponsor and I think Matt had too, but suddenly it was all back on. We probably should have celebrated wildly, but we didn't. The reality that we were going to Guam hadn't sunk in. Besides, we had too much to sort out in order to get things moving again. We had to tell Dilshan as soon as possible. We had to contact Tino Gil and make sure the Guam FA would still have us. We needed to get kits printed with the sponsor's name. Most importantly of all, we needed to get the team ready. I looked up at the TV and saw David Villa was celebrating.

We had nowhere near enough time to get the team ready, but I was infinitely happier to deal with that problem than the lack of a sponsor. It was a challenge I felt equipped to take on – and I'd become accustomed to fighting against the odds.

On the eve of my return to Pohnpei a fortnight later I was in a by-now familiar position: hunched anxiously over a suitcase trying to work out how I was going to fit everything in. Matt and I were about to make the same journey we had made together just over a year ago, but everything had changed. The student pranks and aimless time-wasting were things of the past. The weight of responsibility was evident in both of us and we spent most of the trip working out exactly what we were going to do when we landed. In addition to our coaching headaches, Matt had rented a very expensive video camera and this time he meant business.

'I've drawn up a shot list,' he said, unfolding a ream of typed pages from his pocket. 'These are the people I want to interview and the places I want to film. After all that practice filming you eating corn-flakes it'd be crazy not to take advantage of being in Micronesia.'

As ever, there was no time for jet lag. When your body has no idea what time it is, it's actually quite easy to convince it that it's perfectly OK to be running a football training session in stifling humidity rather than curled up in bed. The Olympic Committee had funded our accommodation. Somehow they had managed to find a two-bedroom flat for the same price as my single room at Nara Gardens on my last stay. We dumped our bags in our new home and went straight to PICS Field, where Dilshan had arranged to assemble the players.

The grass was quite short and looked well cared for, but there were telltale puddles in the goalmouths and in the usual marshy regions on the edge of the penalty boxes. On the other side of the pitch I could see fifteen figures sitting waiting. In the middle I could make out the distinctive Mohican of Dilshan and the others were grouped in their usual formation; next to the captain were Rocky, Charles and Joseph, then Denson, Marvin, Roger and finally Ryan with Brian, Rodrigo, Bob and Robert on the fringes. The players were all dressed in red sleeveless tops. It was odd to see them in red instead of blue. As we approached, we realised they were all wearing Germany shirts. The players fell about laughing. Dilshan, the engineer of the joke, shook my hand.

'We went to Damian from International FC's house for the England–Germany World Cup match. It wasn't on TV here but he has the best internet on the island and found a way to watch it. As soon as I saw Germany destroy you guys I knew we had to get these from Dollar Up!'

Dollar Up was a small convenience store that strangely sold a number of fake football shirts. There seemed to be no rhyme or reason as to which teams were represented in Dollar Up: Barcelona shirts sat next to Marseille, Tottenham and Ivory Coast training tops. Everything was $5 and locals bought whatever took their fancy. Since few of the customers had ever seen any of the teams play, exchanging the Barcelona tops for Accrington Stanley away kits probably wouldn't have affected sales. Only Dilshan and Ryan watched the Champions League games when they were on TV and aspired to be the players whose replica shirts they wore. During my last spell on the island we would sometimes go out to watch games at a bar and bring Rocky or Charles along. They would always enjoy the spectacle but didn't seem interested in players' names or personalities. They also insisted quite sincerely that they were every bit as good as Barcelona or Inter Milan. It seemed that they genuinely couldn't appreciate the difference in class between what they took part in at PICS and what was on the TV screen.

Matt had met several of the players on our first trip, but I planned to introduce him to the rest of the squad. Nothing so formal was necessary. Matt already had Ryan in a headlock and was singing along to Roger's rendition of Shakira's World Cup theme. Matt's confidence and enthusiasm were infectious and I was relieved to see that the group immediately took to him. Towering over everyone with his long blond hair in a ponytail, he looked like a friendly giant as he shook hands with a cowering Rodrigo. When they heard that Matt lived in Los Angeles, the players bombarded him with questions about the bright lights of the USA. Most of them revolved around the attitude of beautiful American women to Micronesian men. Charles Welson cheerfully informed me that he was now a married man. Given Charles's reputation for womanising and attempted womanising, this came as a shock. He explained that for a couple of weeks it had been his duty to stay at home with his wife, but now he was free to come and go as he pleased.

Dilshan told the story of the final of the Pohnpei Premier League, which I had missed. On the evening of the game between the top two, the old, battered floodlights had finally failed, plunging the pitch into complete darkness. With a good crowd in attendance it was essential to get the match completed, so the spectators and players had switched on their car headlights to illuminate the pitch. There had just about been enough light to play and the Island Pit Bulls won easily against International FC and lifted the first Pohnpei Premier League trophy.

As I set the players off on their warm-up I realised I was nervous. I really wanted them to impress Matt, and I needed to be reassured that they were up to the tests they would face in Guam. Dilshan also seemed to be feeling some pressure. He had been sending positive emails during his spell in charge but now he had to prove that things had stayed on track in my absence. The session started brightly, but to my frustration basic errors started to surface and, even worse, the players didn't seem to care. Charles let the ball through his legs into the net from a tame shot and howled with laughter. Roger and Bob started play-fighting, with Bob chasing the younger man across the pitch aiming kung-fu kicks at his backside while they both giggled. We made the game one-touch but the play seemed to get still more ponderous and passes kept missing their intended recipients. I seethed from the sidelines and was relieved to see that Dilshan was also livid. He repeatedly shouted at the players around him and started to put in increasingly physical challenges on opposing players. Joseph stopped running for the ball after a while, complaining that he felt ill, while Bob insisted it was too hot to play. The pace slowed considerably and it was clear that fitness levels were still not high enough.

'That was seriously good,' Matt said as he, Dilshan and I held a post-mortem for the session, sitting on the steps next to the pitch. 'Things have come such a long way.'

'That was the worst we've played in weeks,' Dilshan insisted, shaking his head. 'We've been working really hard but I don't know what was wrong today, that was terrible.'

I wasn't sure whether Matt was trying to spare our feelings. The level had obviously improved hugely from the aimless kickarounds of a year ago, but it needed to progress a great deal further if we were to go to Guam and win. The thing that worried me most was that the players didn't seem to appreciate that. My mood didn't improve on our return to the flat. On first inspection it seemed perfectly acceptable, but when we looked a little closer nothing seemed to work. There was no air conditioning and just one tiny fan, which fought in vain to prevent temperatures soaring. We were sweating within minutes. The beds were just thin boards of wood that creaked worryingly under the weight of a human body. Worst of all, though, the toilet didn't work and that proved to be the final straw. We spoke to the landlady and were relieved when she promised that 'the best plumber on Pohnpei' would come round to fix the toilet immediately. Sure enough, a tired-looking local knocked on our door, nodded politely and set to work. We took the chance to go and get something to eat. We returned two hours later in much higher spirits and opened the door to the bathroom. The toilet had been upended and lay on the floor like a corpse. On the wall was a note that read simply: 'Toilet No Good'. Over the course of the next few days we were forced to

make the two-hundred-metre dash to the Telecom Centre in order
to use their facilities: an arrangement that very quickly began to
seem normal.

After the wake-up call of the first training session back, Dilshan,
Matt and I sat down and drew up a training schedule demanding
an intensity of effort that had never previously been seen in
Pohnpei. We would train five times a week at PICS Field and the
whole team would be expected in the gym at least once a week.

'Can we get this to work?' I asked Dilshan, remembering how
hard it had been to get players to turn up on time for three sessions
every week.

'They'll come, man,' Dilshan said casually. 'The only thing is that
because we train at 4 p.m., we'll need to do the gym early. The best
time is 5 a.m., then nobody has any excuse.'

It wasn't a daunting prospect for Dilshan, who regularly went
up to PICS Field as the sun rose to practise hitting free kicks in the
coolest hours of the day. He had been joined by fellow central
midfielder Nick in recent weeks and the two were now as much
a fixture at PICS as the toads. Having demanded more commitment from the players, we knew we couldn't baulk at the idea of
losing our precious morning lie-in, so we agreed. The next day I
opened my eyes to see Matthew Carlot staring down at me. It took
me a couple of seconds to recognise him, partly because I'd only
ever seen him a handful of times and partly because he'd lost a vast
amount of weight. He looked completely different and had culti-
vated a bushy Afro over the last two months.

'Wakey wakey time,' he grinned.

Since he played against us for the All Stars, Matthew's dad Albert had firmly pushed him and he hadn't missed a single training session with the Pohnpei squad. Furthermore, he'd been going for morning jogs up the steepest hill on the island. In the humidity of Pohnpei you can lose weight pretty fast if you're willing to push yourself. Matthew had been allowed to drive the family car – a shiny new sports utility vehicle that looked out of place on the roads of Pohnpei. He threw a dog-eared copy of the Bible labelled 'SDA School' to the car's floor to allow Matt to sit next to Rocky and Marvin.

During previous stays on Pohnpei I'd gone to the rustic Hideaway Gym, located above the pigpen, with Dilshan on occasion, but few of the other players had ever been there. They were excited at the idea of going. Even though the entrance fee was only $2 and there was very seldom anyone there to collect it, going to a gym was seen as a luxury only foreigners could afford. As we drove up the winding lane next to Hideaway just before 5.30 a.m., the conversation from the back of the car reached my ears.

'I'm going to have big muscles,' Nick was saying. 'Then I'll look like Denson.'

Marvin laughed. 'Maybe if we leave you in there for ten years,' he replied.

Denson was already at the gym waiting for us, having driven there in his taxi. He was wearing a sleeveless top that revealed his enormous muscles. I noticed a cross tattoo that had been carved crudely on his left bicep. The thought of telling Denson how to lift weights made me smile.

Despite the unearthly hour, almost everyone turned up. The absentees were the usual suspects: Bob, Robert and Joseph. Bob and Robert had muttered something about going fishing when the gym was mentioned; Joseph hadn't replied at all. Even Charles, who had started to attend more regularly since his marriage, couldn't say where his brother was. It was past the time for holding players' hands: we could only work with those who wanted to improve.

I demonstrated a circuit of football-specific exercises that I had picked up from lengthy research and my time as a player back in England. I split them up into pairings of roughly similar stature and then walked round to make sure that their technique was good and they weren't trying to lift weights that were too heavy for them. In my sleepy state I was especially grateful to have Matt there. As I stepped in to help Ryan and Marvin, who between them were struggling to lift a 20kg dumb-bell, Matt acted swiftly to prevent Roger from tripping under the squat bar. Roger set the ancient radio to Paradise FM and the volume level steadily increased as Pohnpeian favourites filled the room. After the session had run its course we led a jog from the gym to the Causeway, finishing off with a short sprint as the sun rose over the sea. By 7.30 we were having breakfast, feeling altogether better about the world.

Having Matt around was fantastic. Brimming with energy and not afraid to bark instructions, he was my enforcer. While I set drills and planned sessions, Matt was my right-hand man, refereeing mini-games and starting, watching and announcing the result of every exercise we did. The players warmed to Matt very quickly but also learned that he meant business. If they were late, they could expect to do laps of the pitch as a punishment. If they lost in a drill, they could expect press-ups. I was able to watch and analyse without the pressure of maintaining order and I felt as though Matt and I were a team: I was no longer out on a limb. Dilshan was clearly happier too as he could concentrate on being a player rather than having to be a coach as well. Soon Dilshan playfully started to challenge Matt's authority and duly was given the suitable number of laps around PICS Field. I wondered wistfully what we might have achieved had we both been here for the whole twelve months.

Meanwhile, Matt was also managing to fill the role of session recorder. He would set up the camera on a tripod to capture training routines and then grab players to ask them questions as we finished off the session. Initially the filming had an interesting effect on certain players: Roger would revel in performing feats of acrobatics whenever he was in shot, while Bob would frequently make lewd remarks and giggle at the lens, but Robert froze up whenever he went near the camera. He clearly hated the idea of being filmed. Generally, though, the video footage was a huge help. After sessions we could pick through it to see where things needed more attention and I was hugely impressed by the quality of Matt's work.

The Micro Games were fast approaching and the athletes were running time trials on the track directly alongside the pitch. Out of respect to coaches Michaela and George, we did everything we could to prevent balls flying into the path of runners. Despite Rocky's mumblings that 'this is our fucking pitch, man', we only ran small-scale drills while the track athletes were present. The new arrangement was frustrating but manageable until the arrival of Pohnpei's shot-put representative. There was plenty of grass elsewhere on the island, but he decided that he needed to practise on the corner of the football pitch. We politely tried to suggest other sites, but he was immovable and insisted on heaving the heavy shot into the penalty box at regular intervals during our sessions. For fear of seeing one of our players poleaxed, we coned off the corner of the pitch.

'Don't throw it too far!' Matt joked.

The shot-putter remained steely faced.

We carried on as best we could, but before long we lost still more territory to the long jumpers. The situation had become ridiculous. We were trying to run training sessions in a tiny area of the pitch, which happened to be the most boggy, and lived in fear of a ball hitting any athlete. Matt and I handled things as calmly as possible at PICS but as soon as the car door closed on the journey home we would unleash a torrent of abuse directed at everyone we felt was trying to make our lives even harder than they already were. The only thing for it was to go and see the lieutenant governor, who had always pledged his support to our cause. Churchill had gone up in the world. The new town hall building had been completed and he had traded his governmental tree house for a sparkling office overlooking the ocean. Matt, Dilshan and I nodded at the sleepy security guard and entered the town hall.

'This is the only elevator on Pohnpei,' Dilshan said as we waited for the lift to take us up to the second level of two. 'Everyone got really excited about this!'

Churchill greeted us warmly at the door of his office in his Hawaiian shirt, sipping an iced tea.

'How's the soccer going, then?' he said. 'Are you guys ready to go to Guam?'

We explained our predicament about the pitch.

'You know that I've always been a big fan of soccer,' he said. 'I live next to PICS and I come down and watch you guys all the time.'

In a year, I'd never seen Churchill at PICS.

'So I'm going to help you. The floodlights will be fixed, so then you can play later after the athletes go home. I'll get it done as soon as possible.'

We thanked Churchill effusively but none of us really believed anything would happen. Sure enough, nothing did happen, and our only option was to leave PICS Field. We had scouted out possible alternative sites at various times when the pitch was flooded and unplayable and decided that the rarely used baseball field at the college in Kolonia was the best choice. The drawback of the baseball field was fairly obvious: it was a baseball field. But the grass was shorter than PICS Field, and it had much better drainage and more space. In my whole time on the island I had only seen the pitch used twice for baseball and it was now off-season and deserted except for a few local kids who gathered there to throw stones at each other.

We called Jim Tobin, who said he couldn't see why we wouldn't be able to use the pitch. So we began to train in our new home. The players were having a great time. The ball rolled naturally, which was a huge novelty, and you could make a run down the wing without the imminent threat of a shot-put to the head. Even the neighbourhood kids were on-side and began to cheer their support.

But, suddenly and without warning, a fat shirtless man appeared in the middle of the pitch. He picked up the ball and stood glowering indignantly.

'Who are you? Who said you could use this field?' he demanded.

'This is the Pohnpei State soccer team and they're preparing to tour Guam. They're going to make Pohnpei proud, but we need to train here because PICS is no good.'

'You can't train here. This is the college's field and I say who plays here.'

Matt was furious. I had never seen him this angry. I was pretty sure he was going to knock the guy out. Part of me wanted to see it happen, but I suspected it would probably be a disastrous decision in the long run.

'I understand you're just doing your job and I'm sorry we didn't ask you, but we didn't know,' I ventured. 'Could we at least train here for the rest of the week?'

'Finish up and leave,' he said.

I felt my blood boil. Fortunately, Dilshan pushed Matt and me to one side.

'I know this guy,' he said. 'Nothing good will happen if we insult him.'

Dilshan was the voice of reason. We were unwelcome visitors and had to return to PICS. I glanced at Edwin Sione's office overlooking the field: I had tried to visit Edwin a couple of times to clear the air but he had never been in, and I couldn't help but wonder if he had had anything to do with our speedy eviction.

Given the regularity and intensity of training sessions, there was a need for variation to maintain interest amongst both the players and ourselves. I spent at least an hour every day drafting the next session, trying to conjure up new ideas. As a warm-up we would force players to pass using their heads and watch as their movement off the ball improved. The game we created was similar to basketball and the players' agility was incredible. Tom came into his own but we were astonished to see Micah dispossess him and even

Dilshan repeatedly leaped up to challenge a man almost a foot taller than him.

Basketball star Tom Mawi had returned from representing Pohnpei at the Micro Games in Palau with a typical tale of woe. Pohnpei had been beaten, beaten again and gone home dejected. However, the track and field athletes had done very well. It was no surprise on the island, and especially not to us footballers who had sacrificed our pitch: Pohnpei was good at track and field but bad at team sports, everyone knew that. Tom didn't expect to get a place on the plane to Guam, but he quietly slotted back into the squad, sweated buckets in training and went home, often not saying a word during the whole two-hour session. The massive central defender was a gentle, serene presence but uncompromising on the ball. He could send smaller players like Rodrigo flying with the smallest movement of his arm before picking his stricken opponent up and ruffling his hair apologetically. Tom wasn't quick – in fact he was downright slow – but he stood a foot above our other players, was almost impossible to tackle and unbeatable in the air.

We used American-football drills to improve defensive body position and were stunned to see goalkeeper Brian Taylor, so shy of contact when he was between the posts, throw himself into Denson and flatten him. The two players to stand out in these sessions were unlikely candidates Matthew Carlot and Micah. When others became fatigued, they would be the ones chasing every ball down and both men seemed to have a lethal eye for goal. Micah's main strength was his lack of fear; when he saw the goal he would shoot and it would usually go in. From the penalty spot Micah was unbeatable and would win every competition. While Dilshan's usually impeccable technique fell to pieces under the pressure of taking a penalty kick, it just didn't seem to bother Micah and he was ruthless in his accuracy.

Despite our best efforts to keep training varied, I was starting to tire of some of the drills. Even more, I was starting to tire of the absences. Charles was a regular attender but would more often than not bring the news that Joseph had an ailment that prevented him from coming. And one day, the building frustration over Joseph's lack of commitment came to an inevitable and spectacular head during a practice game with another hastily assembled Island All Star side. The primary aim of the exercise was to see how far we had come as a team since our nervy 2–1 win back in February. The secondary aim was to reward the players who had been working hard in training with a place in the starting eleven to show they were on the right track and to give a jolt to those who had looked complacent.

Having seen Matthew Carlot work tirelessly in pursuit of fitness, we decided it was time to hand him a blue shirt of his own and a place up front. The man to make way was our most naturally talented but least disciplined player, Joseph Welson. Joseph's place in the team had never been in doubt since I first saw him strike a ball, but he had started to take his position for granted. If Joseph *did* turn up to training, he was late, or didn't apply himself – and he always carried himself with a sulky indifference that had gradually worn thin. It was time he realised that nobody's place was guaranteed. While a typically patchy All Star team took it in turns to hoof a ball across the pitch by way of a warm-up, Matt gathered the Pohnpei players into a huddle and we explained the purpose of the match. I said that I was delighted with the effort some players were putting in but needed to see more from others. I made sure not to look at any one player for too long as I said this. A 1–0 win wouldn't be good enough, we needed to play as if we were in Guam. We wanted to win 10–0. Dilshan led a roar of approval and I read out the team.

'And in attack: Ryan and Matthew,' I concluded.

Matthew grinned in surprise. Matt handed him his blue shirt and the rest of the squad applauded – that is with the exception of Joseph, who looked aghast. He was clearly trying to appear unbothered but his quivering top lip gave him away. As the other substitutes left the pitch looking disappointed I touched Joseph on the shoulder.

'You'll be on at half-time,' I told him. 'I want you to be ready to come on and score five.'

Joseph didn't look at me.

The difference in motivation, fitness and technique between the two teams didn't take long to manifest itself. We were 1–0 up within twenty seconds: Dilshan effortlessly dribbled past two All Stars before firing into the corner of the net. He pumped his fist, picked the ball out of the net and ran it to the centre. It was soon 2–0 as Matthew scored his first Pohnpei goal from six yards, and then 3–0 with Dilshan playing in Ryan for a poacher's finish just in time to evade a typically crunching sliding challenge from his dad, Johnson. The improvements we had made over the last few months were visible, but for the first time, they were also audible. For such a long time it had been only Dilshan who would shout on the pitch. The other players were more or less silent, despite our best efforts to encourage them to communicate. But now they were finally talking to each other, calling for the ball and telling teammates who to mark. Even Rodrigo was making himself heard. The shy winger had developed an odd guttural grunt that he would emit whenever he found himself in space.

About fifteen minutes into the game there was a commotion on the sidelines. Edwin Sione had arrived. Edwin had been conspicuous by his absence since we had dethroned him back in August 2009 but there he was bouncing up and down on the sidelines. He had turned up late, unannounced and uninvited, but he was yelling repeatedly at one of the All Stars – a quiet SDA volunteer teacher – to get off the pitch so that he could come on. Eventually the shaken SDA man left the pitch and Edwin raced on, barking incomprehensible orders to his new teammates. He had very little impact on the game. He was clearly trying to make a point and every time an All Star got possession he would hear a high-pitched yell of 'passpasspass now' as Edwin ran in circles like a dog chasing its tail. Each time he did receive the ball, Edwin would dribble as far as he possibly could before trying to shoot.

By half-time it was 5–0, courtesy of a couple of master strokes from Dilshan. The All Stars were starting to get at each other and looked less than pleased to be playing. We gathered the team to give a half-time team talk but there was no Joseph.

'I saw him over by the basketball courts,' Rocky said. 'Shall I go get him?'

Rocky strode off purposefully while Matt and I gave some tactical pointers for the second half. The main thing we wanted was for our lads to show no mercy. Dilshan finished off by demanding a 10–0 win.

'Any less than 10–0 is a loss,' he said.

Rocky had returned without Joseph. He didn't look happy.

'Joseph's quit the team,' he said. 'He said he doesn't want to play any more. I tried to talk to him but he just swore at me and walked off.'

Without a word Charles left the huddle and walked to the

sideline, taking off his shirt and throwing it on the ground. Dilshan called after him but he ambled off, climbing over the fence at the edge of the field and crossing the road. Brian was handed the gloves and a stunned team prepared to restart the game.

The second half was something of an anticlimax after the drama in the break. Marvin scored an excellent goal to make it 6–0, but the All Stars struck back with the best goal of the game: Johnson weaved in and out of our defence, leaving men twenty years his junior standing, and blasted into the roof of the net.

Edwin left ten minutes before the end of the match as suddenly as he'd arrived. It was a Pohnpei corner and he simply jogged off the pitch over to his parked car and drove off. The patient SDA volunteer he had usurped jogged back on.

The game ended 7–1, but the result had been completely eclipsed by the loss of two key players. The others sat, speculating about whether Joseph and Charles would return, while Dilshan, Matt and I held a crisis meeting. The only person who had ever seemed to get through to Joseph was Dilshan. We decided Dilshan would have to go and talk to him.

Trying to restore some positivity, we decided to congratulate the players who had excelled. The first port of call was Marvin, who was sitting some distance from the other players, distractedly playing with his battered mobile phone.

'Great goal today, diamond geezer!' Matt yelled at him. Matt had taught Marvin the phrase 'diamond geezer' and it was now a staple in his vocabulary.

'Thanks, Coach,' Marvin mumbled. He looked like he'd scored an own goal.

'Can I ask something?' he went on. 'Do you think I'd be a good father?'

The question came from nowhere. We offered what we hoped were encouraging noises. Marvin explained that his girlfriend was pregnant. He had only told a handful of people, including Dilshan, because the child would be born out of wedlock. The custom in this situation was to stay silent and for the pregnant woman to stay out of sight until the baby was born.

'My girlfriend will give birth in three months and I don't feel ready to be a dad.'

Marvin looked young for a twenty-year-old. He hardly looked old enough to shave, let alone have a child, but by Pohnpeian standards he was the average age to become a father. The generally lax view on contraception on Pohnpei leads to many teenage pregnancies and it's not at all uncommon to be introduced to someone's uncle and discover they and their nephew are of a roughly similar age. We reassured Marvin as best we could and genuinely believed what we were saying. He was very mature for his age and had a naturally kind and generous nature. He seemed a little happier and went to sit with the rest of the players, who were throwing mud at each other. As Matt approached, Matthew landed a huge clump directly on his forehead. There was uproarious laughter. Matt was clearly amused but pretended to be livid. The laughter stopped as Matt bellowed at a now scared Matthew and ordered him to run ten laps of the track. As Matthew began his first lap, almost in tears, Matt began to laugh and Matthew returned to the group with a rueful smile.

Matt and I kept each other sane as everything around us seemed madder and madder. One evening we decided to treat ourselves by going out to eat – we had set our hearts on tuna steaks so we went to a restaurant next to the marina overlooking the ocean. We sat down and Matt started to place his order but he was stopped mid-flow.

'No fish,' the waitress said with a toothless grin.

'But we walked past a stand loaded with tuna,' Matt said.

'No fish.'

'But there's a fishing boat right there with tuna on it.'

I was on Matt's side, it seemed bizarre that a restaurant over-looking a fishing port couldn't serve us fish, but it wasn't the first time I'd seen this kind of thing. Several times I'd asked for a coconut at a bar only to be offered Sprite instead while coconuts rotted in the trees directly overhead.

An organisation called the Island Food Community often held meetings and visited schools to try and encourage Pohnpeians to cultivate and eat local produce instead of imported fast food. They were fighting gamely, but it was a tough battle. The most popular food for kids at school was the hideous mixture of the sugary drink Kool-Aid and ramen noodles. You would see teenagers add the bright red Kool-Aid to the dry noodles and shovel the revolting mixture into their mouths. While the Island Food Community tried to address these incredibly damaging dietary habits, the convenience and low cost of such 'meals' were hard to tackle. Furthermore, there was still a lingering conception that American food was in some way classy – it was a status symbol.

Matt wasn't in the mood to take no for an answer.

'Wait here,' he said, and he was gone.

Ten minutes later he reappeared with a whole skipjack tuna cradled in his arms. He went into the kitchen and came back to sit down with a satisfied smile on his face. We had our tuna steaks that night.

Despite the months I had spent on the island, life on Pohnpei remained tricky to navigate, and every day was packed full of small tests. While Dilshan seemed to float through life's problems with limitless patience, Matt and I allowed the minutiae to frustrate us. Dilshan sounded like a local and had, consciously or unconsciously, adopted a variety of Pohnpeian mannerisms. He knew when to bow his head slightly as he spoke, he knew when to nod at a passing stranger and who he could call 'nahn' (mate) and who he should call 'maing' (sir). He had even picked up the habit of clapping his hands in front of him as he walked, like the Pohnpeians often did. By contrast, Matt and I were foreign on every level and the harder we tried to fit into Pohnpeian society, the clumsier we seemed. Misunderstandings and awkwardness seemed to follow us around – like the day we made a trip to Pohnpei's cinema. Dilshan was keen to watch *Avatar*, which had finally arrived on the island almost six months after it had taken the US by storm. He and I had been to see films quite regularly during my spells on the island as a ticket cost only $2.

Matt guided the car into a space in the empty car park and switched off the engine. As he did so there was a tap on the window. A bulky security guard wearing an orange shirt and a Montreal Expos baseball cap had appeared from nowhere.

'Can't park here; it's reserved,' he said. 'Please move the car, sir.'

Matt started to swear under his breath but luckily the security guard recognised Dilshan and gestured that we didn't need to move after all.

The evening seemed destined for failure when we entered the

cinema only to find that *Avatar* had started twenty minutes earlier. Dilshan asked the cashier if he could get the film restarted and he agreed. Matt and I were stunned but all became clear when we entered the auditorium and saw *Avatar* playing to a completely empty room.

9

AN INJURY CRISIS

Hafa Adai Matt and Paul,

We have drawn up a schedule that we think will suit your boys. We have three games lined up and everyone is very keen to play against a Pohnpei team. As we don't quite know what level your team is at we propose for you to challenge a Second Division team, then a First Division team (although they have just been relegated!) and a men's national side. Rather than play our full men's nationals it might be better if you take on a team of mostly Under-19s, but you can decide that after the first couple of games.

The players can all stay in our 20-bed dormitory on site at the Guam Football Association facility.

We are all very excited for your visit and are spreading the word amongst the Pohnpeian community on Guam.

Schedule:

Sat. 2 Oct - Rovers 4.00 p.m.

Sun. 3 Oct. - Crushers 4.00 p.m.

Wed. 6 Oct. - Guam National (Under-19) 4.30 p.m.

Tino

The dates had been set and there was no going back now. Although Matt and I had to be primarily focused on events on the pitch, we were aware that the most important appointments in Guam would be the meetings with football officials who would have it in their power to finally make FIFA take note of Pohnpei. We looked at the single-word team names and wondered exactly who we would be up against. There was no information to be had on the internet and we didn't exactly have a network of scouts. There was very little we could do to work out whether we were out of our depth. The games were all very close together and it was obvious that fitness would be key, especially playing at 4 p.m., when the sun would still be hot in the sky. As for the question of playing a full Guam national side or a youth side, Matt and I were strongly questioning the wisdom in leading our fragile-spirited young team out like lambs to the slaughter against a fully fledged senior side. However, any mention of playing anything but a full Guam team met rumblings of discontent in our ranks.

'I understand what you guys are doing, but I've spoken to everyone and we agree that we'd rather lose 20–0 to a full Guam team than play their youth side,' Dilshan told us one evening.

The older, more pugnacious heads such as Rocky were certainly in agreement with Dilshan, but the likes of Rodrigo, Marvin and Ryan were far less vocal on the subject. Matt and I were torn. We had always set out to play a full international and could sympathise with Dilshan's point of view, but we knew as coaches it was our responsibility to protect and nurture our players. While Dilshan, and perhaps Rocky, might be able to laugh off a resounding, embarrassing defeat (and we were far from sure about Rocky), it could extinguish the interest of several more delicate egos. Furthermore, if we returned from Guam the victims of a cricket score, it would be all too easy for our achievements to date to be written off and become another lamentable Wikipedia statistic. Once again Pohnpeians would say, with apparent justification, that locals could never be good at football. Besides, it was hardly as if we would be anything but underdogs against an Under-19 side that had trained as a group since the age of five in Guam's glittering facilities.

That decision could be made later. For now we needed to get the plane tickets in our hands. Since Coyne Airways had agreed to sponsor us, Larry Coyne had made several attempts to pay for the tickets to Guam but had been thwarted by the twin evils of time difference and bureaucracy. The tickets were still on hold for us because of the attempts to pay, but at any point the powers that be could give up on us. Continental Micronesia has one small office at the airport that is open for the two hours around the flights that leave Pohnpei International Airport. On a day-to-day basis the ticketing agents deal with walk-in purchases and the occasional ticket change, so they weren't altogether prepared to deal with two Englishmen trying to book eighteen flights with payment coming from a foreign company.

Over the course of two weeks, we visited the Continental office more or less every day, sitting in the viciously air-conditioned office while the well-meaning staff attempted to complete our booking. Before long we knew every employee at the airport by name and they used the regularity of our visits as a gauge of what time of day it was. We mainly dealt with Rosie – a middle-aged woman with the patience of a saint – who strangely seemed to understand and quite enjoy our very English sense of humour. Rosie was as Pohnpeian as they come. She would sing her words, drawing out the final syllables for almost a minute.

'So, the tickets are for Pohnpei–Guaaaaaaaaaaamm and then Guam–Pohnpeiiiiiiiii.'

The more panic we exhibited at the lack of tickets, the calmer and more jovial she became. She took on a somewhat maternal role towards us and after each ninety-minute conversation would console us that the tickets would arrive eventually. We always asked what the problem was and what we could do to speed things along, but the typically Micronesian answer was always that there was nothing to be done – the tickets would be with us in their own time.

Blissfully unaware of the fact that their tickets to Guam existed only in a theoretical sense, the players continued to make their case for places on the tour.

Robert was a frustrating man to coach. Despite the long hours he spent working on a building site, he would always turn up to training and work hard. He made no secret of how much it meant to him to be in the squad. Having left the island with the last Pohnpeian squad but not been allowed to play a single minute, he was desperate to set things right this time. But while Robert's effort could not be questioned, his performance could be. I'd seen other younger members of the squad like the wild cards Nick and Marvin, and the twins' cousin Rodrigo, transform in front of my eyes into gifted, intelligent players. Robert, on the other hand, had hardly changed at all. He could only really play at right back, but he was regularly caught out of position and still favoured death-or-glory lunges over tracking back and making measured tackles. The idea of watching him play for us in Guam gave me the shivers.

Near the end of one session, Robert was the last man between Ryan and the goal.

'Stay on your feet!' I yelled from the sideline. 'Hold him up.'

Ryan was on the edge of the box and looked up, Robert was bearing down on him at speed.

'Stay on your feet! Stay on your feet!'

Robert threw himself headlong at Ryan's feet. A bemused Ryan tapped the ball ahead of him, hurdled the sliding right back and fired past a stranded Brian.

'I told you to stay on your fucking feet!'

It was the first time most of the players had heard me swear, let alone at someone who was older than me. That was very much a faux pas in polite Pohnpeian society, but this was football and I had been politely trying to smooth the rough edges on Robert's game for a year without any visible impact. I called Robert over, leaving Matt in charge of the game. The players carried on but I could see Nick and Dilshan trying to stop themselves laughing.

'Coach, I'm sorry, Coach, I'm sorry,' Robert said, covering his face with his hand. 'In Guam I'll be different, I promise.'

So much for playing without fear, I thought.

Charles wanted to talk to us. It had been just over a week since he'd followed his brother Joseph off the field and out of the squad. Dilshan had told me that Charles had been hiding behind the stand at PICS watching our training sessions but I hadn't caught sight of him. Alika still hadn't returned, so we were down to one goalkeeper and we were without our best striker. We needed Charles and Joseph but I couldn't go crawling to get them back. What hope would I have of exerting any authority over them if I did? Dilshan had brought Charles in his car to the Telecom Centre, where we had been making use of the facilities. Charles shook my hand and shook Matt's hand but he didn't look us in the eye.

'I'm sorry,' he muttered. 'Joseph's sorry too. He thought there was no way he could go to Guam so he walked off.'

This was obviously very awkward for Charles, so we didn't draw it out. I made it clear that his apology was accepted and, although he hadn't graced us with his presence, so was Joseph's. They would be welcome at training the following day and nothing more would be said about it. The relief was tangible. Sure enough, Charles and Joseph were at training the next day and for the first time in my memory they had made the hundred-metre trek from their house on time. Charles was his usual gregarious self but in his absence he had perfected a 'concentration face' that he pulled whenever Matt or I was talking. Joseph celebrated his return to training by scoring a hat-trick in a practice game. He still didn't smile or speak to me but he nodded when spoken to, which was a definite breakthrough.

Eight weeks before the tour was due to start, it was time for me to leave once more. I needed to return to England to pick up the new Coyne Airways Pohnpei shirts as well as the regulation shorts and socks that the players would have to finally wear. We had ordered XXL for all the shorts to cater for their island sensitivities. The shipping charge to get them delivered to Pohnpei would have been more than the cost of the kit order itself. Matt was needed in LA to formally collect his degree certificate and tie up various odds and ends he had left loose in his haste to return to Micronesia. Generally it takes a month just to get over the culture shock of leaving Pohnpei, but we would have just three weeks before we returned to the island.

Roger had insisted that we have a farewell meal at his house. His parents wanted to show their gratitude to us for taking him to Guam. Given Roger's personality and his secure place in the team, we didn't have to worry that the meal might be interpreted as a bribe to influence squad selection. We happily accepted. Roger lived some way from town in the district of Nett. From PICS we drove for five minutes on the main road before turning down a pitch-black lane. The road continued, winding past the prison where Bob and Robert famously spent the night and into deeper and deeper jungle. Every now and again a fierce dog would threaten to attack the car door. Small children appeared from nowhere before disappearing back into the undergrowth. Roger had made this long journey on foot every day before we had begun taking him home in the car. Eventually we arrived at what looked like a large tent where a huge number of people were sitting in a circle, heads flopped in a telltale sakau trance.

As we entered the tent Roger formally introduced us to the Nakasone family, keeping his head bowed the entire time. Roger's father sat shirtless and grey-haired at the head of the circle. He didn't move as we shook his hand, bowed and offered him a 'kaselehlie'. We were shown to two seats on the periphery and told that we must help ourselves to food. It was a feast. Roger guided us round the table, offering us the different dishes: bread-fruit, chicken wings, ribs, tuna, white fish, plantain and taro. Nervous under the scrutiny of the seated family members, we accepted everything, piling our plates high. Roger thanked us for eating the food.

'I'm sorry it's not much,' he said.

Roger's family was by no means rich and we knew that the custom for such a meal was to put more food on the table than the family would eat in a month – and to apologise for not producing enough. They would have spent all the money they had, and killed a prized chicken. The family refused to eat until we had finished. Eventually we managed to satisfy the Nakasones that we were full and very happy and they began to eat while the sakau continued to do the rounds.

Roger was an anomaly. He'd always proudly told us that he was 'substance free'. He wouldn't drink, smoke, chew or partake of sakau, and I had presumed this was a family ethos. In fact, the Nakasones were respected as one of the greatest sakau producers on the island.

The sakau was being served from a coconut shell. We took as small sips as we could and passed it around, but the hosts ensured that it would come back in our direction very quickly. We complimented the sakau fifty times. Nobody seemed to notice. After our fifth sip of sakau, Roger tapped us on the shoulders and explained that it would be polite to leave, so we effusively thanked Roger's father, who was more or less asleep. We left and breathed a sigh of relief.

Back in the UK, our supplier had made a mistake with the order and the Pohnpei shirts for the tour weren't going to be ready for a month. As problems go it wasn't a huge one. I called Matt in Los Angeles and we agreed that he would go back to Pohnpei as planned and I would follow on a couple of weeks later with the kit. We trusted Dilshan would be able to keep things in order but

I was sure he'd appreciate having Matt around as soon as possible to keep the players from slacking. A pleasing consequence of being kept waiting for the shirts was that I got to spend some more time with Lizzie. We left London to spend a few days in Gloucestershire at her mum's house, and in the peace and quiet of the countryside I was able to recharge my batteries for the final push. For two blissful days I did nothing football related except occasionally scribbling formations, tactics and ideas for drills in a notepad. Pohnpei felt a very long way away. Early on the third morning Lizzie's mum knocked on the door and handed me the phone. It was Matt – and he had some terrible news about Joseph.

Joseph had been run over by a drunk driver. He had a broken pelvis and two broken legs, and it was touch and go whether he'd live. It had happened at PICS Field, just yards from where we trained. Joseph had been sitting with a group of friends watching a basketball match when a car came round the bend going far too fast. It swerved too late and hit Joseph. The driver had stopped momentarily and been confronted by a hysterical Charles before he sped off into the distance. Joseph was rushed to hospital in excruciating pain. Dilshan and several other players kept a vigil by his bedside, even though the sight of their teammate shoddily bandaged and in evident agony must have been hard to bear. The doctors were doing their best for Joseph but Pohnpei's medical facilities really weren't up to the task. There was no hope that Joseph's family could transfer him to one of the far superior hospitals off-island. The Welsons had little money and no status: they were simply an average Pohnpeian family. Joseph's uncle Welbie seemed unable to comprehend the severity of the injuries, and while Dilshan tried to explain how bad things were, Welbie insisted that Joseph would make a full recovery in due course.

I waited by the phone for news. Dilshan called with an update a day later and told us that Joseph's condition was deteriorating. The drunk driver had come forward, but he wouldn't be facing criminal charges as he had 'come to an arrangement' with the family in the Pohnpeian custom. The driver had visited Joseph's family to apologise and offered a sum of money to make things right. The Welsons had to accept; to refuse his offer would have put them in the wrong. I was told by a number of people on the island that, according to tradition, someone who committed murder on Pohnpei could be forgiven if they took part in a ceremony that involved them crawling on their hands and knees and asking for forgiveness. While these days the courts were usually used instead to determine justice, the old traditions had by no means died out.

Charles was in a bad way. He blamed himself for his younger brother's injury. He'd just gone home from PICS when he heard the crash. In the aftermath of the collision, Charles had punched the driver and had been kept away from negotiations with the family. It became clear that Joseph's only hope of survival was to leave the island. While he didn't have powerful friends or a religious group to rally round, he had the football community, and Ryan's dad Johnson used his influence to exert pressure on the government to come to Joseph's rescue. Micronesia has an agreement with the Philippines that allows important islanders to be flown to Manila for treatment in some of the world's best hospitals. Amazingly, the government agreed to pay for Joseph to be treated there, so long as he could find the fare.

Joseph's ticket to Manila was funded by a whip-round amongst the island's footballers. However, the terrified teenager had never been away before and was convinced that he wouldn't survive such a journey into the unknown. He would only leave the island if his uncle Welbie could come with him. But there was no more money to pay for a second ticket. The solution came at the eleventh hour in the form of Walden Weilbacher. Pohnpeian expat Walden ran a Guam-based charity called the Ayuda Foundation, set up to help Micronesians abroad. By coincidence, he had emailed Matt and me to ask whether we needed any assistance with our tour of Guam. Matt pounced on the opportunity and replied to ask whether he could assist with a plane ticket for Welbie instead. It was a shot in the dark, but it worked. Walden had booked Welbie a ticket within two days and Joseph was able to fly. There was little news once Joseph arrived in Manila. It was a terrifying wait, and after just under a week Dilshan received a call – Joseph was much better. He was awake and on morphine but had undergone successful surgery. He faced a long road of rehabilitation but he would recover. The doctors had no doubt that, left in Pohnpei, he would have been paralysed or worse. Dilshan delivered the news to me over the phone. I fought back tears of relief and heard him doing the same.

'We're going back to training,' he said. 'The guys want to make Joseph proud.'

The first thing Matt saw at PICS Field on his return were two broken mini-football goals. The bars had been snapped off their frames in what seemed to be a random act of vandalism. Like any great detective, Matt delved deeper, looking for clues, and found a lead. On the evening the goals were broken, Edwin Sione had been seen at PICS Field with several members of the wrestling team he coached. Dilshan confirmed that Edwin had been demonstrating wrestling moves on the goals earlier in the week when he turned up for training. This was compelling circumstantial evidence. Already in a sour mood, Matt was tipped over the edge when the players turned up for training. After Dilshan's stirring email describing a squad fighting for their fallen teammate, Matt had high expectations that it seemed had been dashed.

From: Matthew Conrad
To: Paul Watson

I know 5 a.m. fitness sessions are not appetising, but don't say you'll come and then not. To be fair we had to drag Charles out of bed but he tried when he was there.

The work ethic was pretty impressive but that was this morning and a totally different team turned up in the afternoon. Everything went fine until we played attack v defence, when the attack just waited for the ball to come to them. The movement was crap and I had to dole out a lecture.

In the final game, they just started to dick around. I sat them all down and told them that it wasn't good enough and if they couldn't do a push-up without making a song and dance they could just go home. A lot of people were watching and I thought that if they messed around like this and we lost in Guam everyone would say it was because they didn't train hard enough, which hasn't been the case. I pulled the Watson card and they all apologised!

I'm a bit worried about Dilshan. He didn't seem himself so I spoke to him after the session and he told me that he's having some problems with his girlfriend. Just about the worst timing ever.

We've got everything we need here except the kits but if you
want to bring some Marmite with you then I won't stop you.
Can't wait for you to get here geez!

Ever since Joseph's accident I had felt that I was in the wrong
place. I should have been in Pohnpei. Waiting for news of Joseph
had been agony and now it felt like I was neglecting my duties,
impatiently waiting for the arrival of the kit. I asked Matt to tell
the players that we would be doing a bleep test on the day of my
return to send a clear message that there was no time to mess
around.

For those lucky enough to be uninitiated in the art of the bleep
test, it is a physically and mentally draining ordeal designed to test
your cardiovascular abilities. Participants are required to run
between two lines spaced twenty metres apart each time they hear
a bleep on an audio track. At first this is easily done, but the bleeps
get steadily closer together, so as you get more tired you have to
work harder. Each twelve bleeps is a stage and there are, theoreti-
cally at least, twenty stages. The standard requirement for a semi-
professional footballer is to reach Stage 13, but it always becomes
a competition between players, with nobody wanting to be the
first to give in. I once saw a player throw up on Stage 14 while
completing a lap, wipe his mouth and continue to Stage 16 as if
nothing had happened.

I wanted a similar level of dedication from my boys, but if possible with slightly less projectile vomiting. Perhaps foolishly, I
decided that I would up the stakes still further by running the
bleep test with them. No self-respecting Pohnpeian would allow
his pale English coach to outdo him on home soil. I had been
keeping in reasonable shape during my time at home but needed

to take things further, so one afternoon I set out two cones on Ravenscourt Park and ran between them until I couldn't stand any more. It reminded me of the arduous physical work I did prior to my first trip to Pohnpei, terrified of trying to coach players who were fitter than me. As I packed my stuff away shaking and drenched in sweat, an ageing dog walker came up to me and asked what I was training for. I told him it was a long story.

The burning feeling in my lungs started much earlier than I had expected. You can prepare as well as you like on a chilly day in West London, but running in Micronesia is a bit like running in a greenhouse with a sprinkler on. Matt was in charge of the timer. We had a CD of the test but nothing to play it on, so Matt had the track on his iPod and was blowing a whistle at each bleep. Between whistles he was cheering everyone on wildly and had taken to baiting the players who looked close to stopping with comments like 'Come on, Robert, you can't be less fit than your coach!'

Matthew Carlot fought heroically. Not long ago he was more than a stone over a healthy weight, now he looked lean and determined. His dad Albert stood in the distance, watching. However, after Stage 7, Matthew started to tie up. I was certain he was going to stop. Matt focused all his attention on the struggling striker and talked him out of quitting, like a police negotiator talking a man down off a ledge. Miraculously, Matthew found a hidden source of energy and carried on to Stage 12. One by one the players dropped out. At first I had roared encouragement, as had Dilshan, but now it was each man for himself. To speak was to waste breath you wouldn't get back. Bob didn't get to the line in time, Matt slapped him on the back and handed him some water. Robert stopped a lap later. He'd clung on to win bragging rights but he looked decidedly off colour.

Rodrigo pulled up at Stage 14, Nick and Dilshan went at Stage 15, leaving Roger, Ryan and me. At this stage we were all ignoring our bodies yelling at us to stop. This wasn't about physical fitness as much as mental fortitude and Ryan was showing an abundance. The end was something of an anticlimax as we all missed the bleep somewhere around Stage 18 and couldn't catch up again. It was over. We desperately tried to catch our breath and there was a lot of backslapping and hand shaking. Matt took me to one side with a slight grin.

'Look at this,' he said, gesturing at his iPod.

'What?'

All I could see was an iPod. It seemed to be switched off.

'The battery went almost as soon as we started so I timed it in my head and blew the whistle!'

I couldn't help but laugh.

'Let's not tell them, though,' Matt said as the players walked round comparing scores and glowing with pride. 'After all, this is mostly a mental test, you said it yourself.'

Dilshan's body language was all wrong. He had always looked like a leader, whether in training or in a game, but even before the bleep test he had his shoulders slumped and hardly made eye contact with anyone. I wondered how bad things had become with his girlfriend.

Albert Carlot was amongst the players, handing out bottles of water and offering congratulations. Ryan told me that the qualified referee had been almost ever present since we left the last time. He was always there to provide lifts, collect balls and referee matches. It had crossed my mind briefly that it could all be a political push to ensure his son got a place on the plane to Guam, but I reprimanded myself for such cynicism. Even before Matthew had become a member of the squad Albert had given of his time generously. He was a nice bloke who loved football; it was as simple as that.

Matt had looked unusually tired and worried when he'd met me off the plane. He'd had an awful lot to deal with while I was away, but when he saw the beautiful, personalised new shirts with the Coyne Airways logo he brightened up. The blue and white Adidas shirts were eclipsed only by the magnificent black and gold goalkeeping strip. When I slipped face first in a mud puddle within minutes of being back in Pohnpei, he brightened up even more.

'I can't believe I wasn't filming that,' he said. 'Can you do that again?'

But there were serious issues that had to be resolved. All the cash that had been earmarked for food and other everyday expenses in Guam had been spent on getting Joseph to safety. There was no time to find more money and we couldn't ask the football community for additional help. Our only port in this storm was, as usual, Jim Tobin.

'You know that Walden Weilbacher is on the island for a fishing competition?' Jim asked.

We weren't aware of that, but Walden regularly returned to Pohnpei to indulge his passion for fishing. We had seen pictures of him in the local paper proudly holding up unfeasibly big fish. Walden had been the hero when Joseph was in trouble, but surely we couldn't ask him to help out again?

'Walden and I go way back. Let me give him a call.' Jim was already dialling.

It amazed me how quickly things could happen in Pohnpei, even if they so rarely did. Walden had a window of an hour before he set out for the competition. He was with us in ten minutes. The door to Jim's office swung open and Walden walked in. He was tall and well dressed in a smart black shirt and expensive-looking jeans. Walden looked like a visitor from Guam rather than a local, and seemed like a man who was rarely not smiling. Jim explained the situation and stated his belief that the Pohnpeian community in Guam should be responsible for looking after our team during the tour. Walden countered by asking why the Olympic Committee couldn't put up some money. Jim insisted that they would be providing some funding; just not all of it. This was news to us. An odd game of charitable one-upmanship began while Matt and I sat back and smiled at each other. The more Jim offered to help us, the more Walden seemed able to do. Within ten minutes, the NOC had provided a kitty of $750 and Walden had promised that the Pohnpeian community would feed the team for the entirety of their stay. Walden said that we could count on passionate support during our games and that a different Pohnpeian community group would drop by with food for the team every afternoon and evening.

All that remained to be done was to announce the final squad. It might seem slightly cruel, but we had kept the players in the dark about the size of the touring party until now, two weeks before our departure, and for a very good reason. The injury to Joseph had left us with fifteen players competing for sixteen places. If the players had known that, their attitude towards training would have been complacent, to say the least. We had simply told everyone to get passports in case they were selected and Dilshan had babied them through the process of securing the crucial document. The players were all lined up in the goalmouth ready to hear their fate. Only Micah hadn't turned up. We had told everyone that today was selection day and he may have feared rejection after his past indiscipline. Some players looked assured and calm. Rocky, Dilshan, Nick and Ryan were chatting casually. They probably knew as well as we did that to not pick any of them would be lunacy. But Matthew looked nervous, Robert was staring intently at the ground, and Charles, even though in Alika's absence he was more or less guaranteed a place by default, wasn't his usual brash self. Tom was reluctant to line up and hadn't put his boots on. He was ready to quietly slip away.

I began to read out the squad.

'Dilshan. Nick. Ryan. Rocky …'

After each name there was a brief moment of applause before the other players returned to their own personal apprehension.

'Roger. Marvin. Rodrigo …'

Roger grinned and hugged Marvin. Rodrigo did a small skip of celebration but quickly stopped himself from any further reaction as he felt Bob and Robert's eyes on him.

'Denson. Brian. Charles …'

Charles couldn't contain himself. He let out a whoop of joy and came over to hug Dilshan, Matt and me.

'Tom. Bob and Robert …'

Robert made a quick joke in Pohnpeian but was clearly emotional. Bob seemed unbothered.

'And finally, Matthew. Oh, and if anyone sees Micah can you tell him he's going to Guam?'

There was a massive cheer. Matthew punched the air and was given a high-five by Ryan.

'Can you definitely all get time off work and college to come?'
I asked.

There was a ripple of laughter. I had meant it as a serious
question.

Marvin, our father-to-be, looked doubtful, but in private reassured me that he would be on the plane. His girlfriend's due date
was in November, a few weeks after the tour was set to finish.
Within ten minutes Micah had mysteriously appeared and was
wearing a lop-sided smile.

'Thank you,' he said in the direction of Matt and me.'Thank you.'
It was the first time I had heard him speak English.

We decided to hand out the kits and boots. One by one each
player located his personalised blue and white shirt, looked disbe-
lievingly at the name on the back and then quietly retreated with
it. It was hard to tell what was going through their minds. Ryan
immediately bounced up to me to say thank you and a beaming
Roger instructed me to 'thank England very much', but the others
stayed silent and Bob even asked if he could get another shirt
because his was too big. After everyone else had retreated with
their kit, towering defender Tom slowly opened up the bag and
gave a soft grin as he saw a pair of massive size-fourteen boots
waiting for him – the product of many hours trawling eBay. He
laced them up and gingerly walked over to me.

'Thank you, Coach,' he said in a barely audible mumble. 'This
is the first pair of football boots I've ever had that are nearly big
enough.'

I was amazed to finally hear Tom speak a full sentence and was
surprised by how softly spoken he was.

I noticed that most of the players had tucked their shirts away
in their bags rather than putting them on.

'They don't want to ruin them,' Dilshan said. 'For a lot of these guys it's the most expensive thing they've ever owned. Marvin told me he wanted to wear it to his wedding and I don't think he was joking.'

We gathered the players' full names, places and dates of birth on a piece of paper and went home. Matt unfolded the paper in the car and began to laugh.

'It's not Mi-cah,' he explained. 'It's Mik-e. Or in English, Mike.'

Some of the players had struggled to remember their birth dates. I'd stifled a laugh when I saw Robert, still a little emotional, stare blankly at the paper for some time before looking at Bob's entry above and copying his date of birth. After another trip to our second home, the Continental Airlines ticket office, we finally had the tickets printed and showed them to the players. There was a buzz of excited conversation.

'Mr Roger Nakasone,' I could hear Roger say. 'Roger Naka-s-one.'

Matt and I went to get the balls and cones out of the back of the car and became aware that Rodrigo had followed us. He didn't look comfortable, but he never did when called upon to speak.

'It's not my name,' he said, pointing at the ticket with 'Mr Rodrigo Matamba' printed on it.

'What?' Matt boomed. Rodrigo shrank back.

'It's Ratrico Madamba. That's how it says on my passport.'

'But we asked you to write your name on paper and you wrote Rodrigo Matamba.' Matt was incredulous.

I stood in stunned silence.

'Everyone calls me Rodrigo, so I say I'm Rodrigo. But it's Ratrico. And I have trouble with "d" and "t".'

We had to throw ourselves at the mercy of Rosie. She had

warned us in no uncertain terms that the names needed to be spelt correctly when we confirmed them and we had felt we were on safe ground, but now we had a ticket with both forename and surname incorrect. Continental policy said tickets couldn't be transferred. By the letter of the law they could charge us again. Rosie thought about the problem for a little while. Matt was shifting in his seat and I felt a bead of sweat trickle down the back of my neck despite the Arctic air conditioning. Rosie's co-worker giggled.

'Ooooooookkkkkkkkkkkaaaayyyy,' Rosie sang. 'So it's Ratrico not Rodrigo and Madamba not Matamba. All done.'

And just like that she printed the ticket, telling us to ignore the printout attached that said 'NAME CHANGE FEE: $200'.

The final training game before we set off for Guam was an unfocused affair. Nobody could concentrate on anything. Whenever the ball left the pitch players would start to chat about Guam. It was impossible to keep their minds on the task at hand and equally tough for us. Worse still, Dilshan was as good as absent. After all the build-up to the tour, all the rallying of the players, all the training sessions in the driving rain, he had been mentally drained on the eve of our departure.

'I've broken up with my girlfriend,' he told us as we arrived at PICS. 'I don't really want to talk about it at the moment but I'm not going to let it bother me, I swear.'

It was easier said than done. Quite understandably, Dilshan was unrecognisable on the pitch. He was making rare sloppy mistakes, became sullen and disheartened when he missed a chance and had even started to shout at other players for small errors.

The game meandered towards its conclusion. The light was fading and the toads were starting to reclaim the pitch. Micah-who-was-now-Mike bolted down the wing at pace and looked for another player wearing a yellow bib. He spied Dilshan arriving in the middle of the box and whipped over a tantalising cross. Brian was in goal for the non-bibs. We'd been practising exactly this situation for weeks. The keeper called, rose above the strikers and seemed set to bring the ball under his control when he suddenly collapsed to the floor.

Ominously the crowd of players around Brian started to move away. I sprinted in from the sideline. Brian was awake but groggy. Not for the first time I wished that there was someone qualified in sports medicine on the island. He couldn't remember what had happened. Something had hit him in the head – that was all he knew for certain. It looked like a concussion but there was no doubt we had to be safe, so Matt drove Brian to the private health clinic Genesis. Genesis had a better reputation than the Pohnpei State Hospital where Joseph had been treated. Foreigners with insurance policies would pull up to the clinic's bright pink door whenever they had a minor problem and as a teacher at the SDA School, Brian had a rock-solid insurance policy and would be well looked after.

But when I turned up later, Matt looked worried. Brian had experienced some kind of fit. The injured goalkeeper was connected up to a staggering number of drips and was clearly in pain as well as scared. Over the next few hours he just seemed to get worse. The doctors were puzzled. Johnson had brought an army of SDA volunteers to Genesis and they sat by Brian's bedside trying to lighten his mood. All Brian kept saying was that he wanted to play in Guam. We knew that wasn't going to happen but refrained from telling him that while he was in such a fragile state.

As head teacher of SDA School, Johnson threw himself into action on Brian's behalf. A trusted doctor flew in from Guam and inspected Brian. He diagnosed a concussion but also stated that Brian had probably been given two conflicting drugs, inadvertently causing a serious allergic reaction. He recommended that Brian be flown to Guam immediately so he could look after him properly. The insurance company gave the green light within a day and Brian flew to Guam where, ironically, he would be able to play no part in the tour. Now Charles was our only goalkeeper. We had just a handful of days to find a back-up or a ticket would go to waste. We were discussing our problem up at PICS Field when Denson walked up to us.

'You know, I used to be a goalkeeper,' he said. 'I'm not saying I really want to, but if we are desperate I can play in goal.'

I had noticed Denson's skills in goal when he was messing around before training but didn't realise he had serious experience. Denson explained that, during his teenage years in Guam, he had been a decent goalkeeper but he had gone off the rails. His final game on the island had ended in embarrassment – a heavy defeat brought about because he wasn't in a fit state to play. They had been tough times for Denson, who in the past had often come up on the wrong side of the law. He was now a changed man and credited his children for having changed him.

Denson would be a good last resort, in case Charles got injured in Guam, but we needed the big man too much in defence to consider giving him the gloves. There was only one man left to call: Alika.

Alika had stopped playing entirely after the death of his mother. I had bumped into him here and there but there was no question of him pulling the goalkeeping gloves on again. The benefit of calling Alika was that we would be able to kill two birds with one stone. The players, many of whom were teenagers away from home for the first time, were going to stay in a 20-bed dormitory in Guam. They really needed chaperoning, but there was no way Matt and I should be in there. We would lose our sanity, for one thing, and the players would feel they were constantly under scrutiny. Alika was slightly older than most of the players. He was very popular with the squad and had been to Guam on countless occasions. He could be our 'team manager' – our eyes in the dormitory to make sure things didn't get out of control. He was also our reserve goalkeeper, which was in effect just a title. We didn't really expect him to keep goal. And, as it turned out, Alika certainly didn't expect to play.

'For a start, I haven't played soccer in six months,' he said. 'On top of which, I suffer from arthritis and it's gotten worse lately. Basically, if you want me to look after the guys then I'm all good, but if you want me on the pitch I'm pretty much useless.'

We went off to ask Rosie for one last favour.

On my visit to Guam, Tino had given me a stack of DVDs of Guam's national team in action. There was footage of their 1–0 win over the Northern Mariana Islands, their 1–0 triumph over Mongolia and their draw with Macau. We treated these as surveillance tools, studying them for any signs of weakness. It was hard to glean anything useful. Guam looked like a well-organised physical side that would take no prisoners.

We decided to show our players the DVDs, hoping to inspire rather than terrify them. Johnson and his wife invited the team over for a meal with Guam v. Northern Mariana Islands as the entertainment. While Dilshan and Ryan watched with studious expressions, Charles had less respect for the opposition.

'Guam are no good,' he said, leaning back in his chair in contempt. 'We can beat them any day.'

There were grunts of agreement from Mike and Rocky. After the game had finished, we put on a different DVD, which I had brought from home. It was the 2010 World Cup Final – Spain v. Holland. The players watched the action unfold with little excitement. Charles started to fidget and listened to some music on his headphones. By half-time only Dilshan, Denson, Ryan and Nick were watching.

'What do you think of the game?' Dilshan asked the group. 'Can you see the movement of the players and the speed of the passing?'

There were a few shrugs.

'Looks pretty much the same,' Robert piped up.

'The same as Guam v. Northern Mariana Islands?'

'Yep.'

There were murmurs of assent.

It was the final day before the tour. We had gathered the players for a trip to Sokehs Rock, the highest peak on the island. Sokehs Rock was the site of the Sokehs Rebellion in 1910, when the local Pohnpeians rose up to fight their German rulers. The heroic resistance ended in defeat and many Pohnpeians died, but the episode is still viewed with some pride by islanders, as a chapter of defiance in a history of subjugation and passivity. The aim was to instil more national pride in the players ahead of the tour. For Matt and me it was a time for reflection on what would happen after the tour of

Guam. In the frenzied build-up to the trip we hadn't had a lot of time to consider what we would do afterwards, but as we looked over the island with all the preparations completed, we finally started to talk about the future.

'It's the beginning of the end,' I said, watching a plane landing at the airport in the distance.

'I've been thinking that too,' Matt agreed. 'After Guam we can't keep coming back here. We'd either have to move here for good or walk away. You can't keep going backwards and forwards.'

'If the tour goes well and the Guam FA are impressed, then progress will continue once we're gone. And I know Dilshan can take care of things.'

Neither of us wanted to vocalise how much we would miss the place.

As we climbed the track towards the island's summit, remnants of another conflict lay partially hidden in the bushes. The Japanese used Sokehs Rock as a defensive position during their occupation of Pohnpei during the Second World War and their artillery guns were still to be seen, rusting slowly in the undergrowth. Amazingly, most of the players told us that they had never been to Sokehs Rock and seemed surprised by the beauty of the scenery. A football accompanied us everywhere and Dilshan, Nick and Rocky formed a circle to do kick-ups overlooking the town of Kolonia hundreds of metres below. I looked round to see Roger doing a back flip off the guns of a rusted Japanese tank.

It was business as usual at Pohnpei International Airport. The stocky security guard with unfeasibly big biceps ran a roll of cellophane tape around a cool box, probably containing fish. A group of locals sat looking disinterested, each with their own cooler containing essentials for their trip to Guam. A couple of white guys stood awkwardly wearing the traditional leaving gift of a headdress of wild flowers that had either been lovingly woven by the matriarch of a Pohnpeian family or been hastily purchased at the small airport gift shop while the visitors' backs were turned. An elderly Micronesian man broke off mid-anecdote and nodded towards the entrance. Two bickering children fell silent. The white guys took advantage of the distraction to remove the garlands from their heads. And in walked an army of blue and white shirts.

Island time had been forgotten for a day of this magnitude. Every player was on time; in fact, most were early. Rocky had turned up at Dilshan's house six hours before the flight was due to depart. He could have walked to the airport and back ten times before check-in opened.

Our squad made up the majority of the check-in queue. Dilshan, Matt and I split up so that we could assist those players making their first plane journey, which was most of them. Each player had to open his case as he reached the bulky security guard. As Denson opened his the guard gave a red-toothed grin at the contents. A third of Denson's luggage was clothing, the rest was taken up with sakau powder and betel nut. Before setting off we had made it clear that we expected the players to behave like professionals. There would be no chewing betel nut, no smoking and no drinking while we were at the Guam Football Association facility. Of all the people we might have expected to break team rules, Denson was amongst the least likely. Although neither substance was illegal, packing them was strictly against our instructions.

'Don't worry, guys,' he explained. 'I'm bringing this to give to my cousins so they can sell it. You can't get proper sakau or betel nut in Guam, so the Pohnpeian community pays a fortune for it. I can make a month's salary like this.'

If it had been Bob or Robert carrying contraband we would probably have been suspicious of this explanation, but in Denson's hands it just seemed like honest entrepreneurialism. Still, you had to wonder what other fringe benefits our players were hoping to enjoy from this unexpected trip to Micronesia's Las Vegas.

By the time we had completed check-in, a sizeable crowd of relatives had gathered. Matt and I were introduced to two Pohnpeian women in traditional flowery dresses. They were Mike's aunts and they didn't seem to speak any English. Mike stood sheepishly next to them, clutching his plane ticket to his chest, and spoke to them in Pohnpeian.

'Thank you,' one of the women said and grabbed Matt in a tight embrace before also squeezing the breath out of me. 'Mike's a good boy.'

The other woman was carrying a toddler. She handed him to Matt, who feared momentarily he had been given an odd leaving present. Then she removed two flowery headdresses from her bag and placed them on our heads. Jim Tobin arrived and went round shaking each of the players by the hand.

'Can I say a few words before you go?' he asked.

We sat all the players down around the feet of the giant Jim.

'You are all getting an incredible opportunity today,' Jim said. 'You are going to Guam to represent Pohnpei, to represent Micronesia, your country. Everything you do reflects on this island, so be courteous, be professional and be sporting. When you come back you will be the leaders of this sport. Pohnpei is proud of you all, make Pohnpei proud.'

Johnson had driven down to wish his son and his nephew luck. Rocky's father sat silently, seemingly in a stupor, occasionally beckoning his son closer and whispering something to him. Alika had struck up conversation with some girls he knew from the College of Micronesia. We had also received several supportive emails from people in England who had attended the comedy fundraiser and, touchingly, a message from Charles Musana saying how proud he was of what had been achieved.

In the midst of the chaos, we heard a familiar greeting.

'Matty, Paul, geezers!' It was Shepherd's Bush Steve. 'I don't want to get in the way with all the goodbyes and that, but just wanted to say all the best, boys. You give those Guam boys one hell of a beating. We'll have a few drinks when you get back.'

Albert Carlot had gone one step further than the other well-wishers and was coming to Guam to watch the final two games of the tour. He'd been due in Guam for a meeting later in the month and had managed to switch the dates so he could watch Matthew in action. As we got on to the tarmac, Robert walked up alongside Matt and me and handed us each a piece of coral with a string threaded through it.

'These are for good luck,' he said. 'You have to wear these round your necks and then we will win. It's a Pohnpeian charm.'

The flight was like any other to Guam in that it took just under two hours and was bisected by a bumpy landing in Chuuk. While Matt and I sheltered in the air-conditioned cabin during the Chuukese interval, the players filed out of the plane so they could take photos, flirt with airport officials and generally make a nuisance of themselves. When we arrived in Guam we had the tough task of explaining to surly US passport control officials what exactly we had planned for our stay. Denson was on hand to translate the questions for a bemused Mike and a terrified Rodrigo.

'What's in the bags?' an official asked Charles sleepily.

'Soccer kit,' Charles replied with a satisfied grin. 'We're here to beat Guam.'

The official broke into a smile.

'I hope you guys do win. Those Guam soccer players think they're better than they are; take them down!'

The Guam FA's facility must have been a huge culture shock to our players, but it was one they seemed to take in their stride. As we arrived, two of Guam's top teams, Shipyard and Quality, were locked in battle. The pace of the game was intense and the challenges brutal. A crowd of at least 200 had gathered and we were told that there was no love lost between the sides – three men had already been sent off. Rocky was barely able to sit still, he was so desperate to be on the field. Marvin and Ryan were less bullish.

'These guys play pretty hard, eh?' Ryan mumbled.

'This is what we were preparing for. This is why we've been training hard and toughening up,' Dilshan pointed out.

'Yeah, fuck these guys. I'm going to break their legs,' Rocky bragged with a sly smile.

It didn't take long for one of our squad to break team rules – and it was the most predictable of culprits. Training time arrived and there were only fifteen Pohnpei players waiting. Robert was missing.

'Has anyone seen Robert?'

Silence. It was obvious who to ask.

'Bob, where's Robert?'

'I dunno,' he mumbled into the ground. 'He said he'd be here. He went off someplace.'

That was all we could get out of Bob. Dilshan had already started to warm the players up, jogging a steady lap of one of the three perfectly mown pitches. While Matt and I spat venom about Robert on the sideline, Dilshan led the stretches. He looked every bit the captain once more.

Tino had come to watch us train. I felt the pressure as he shook my hand.

'So these are your boys, then,' he said. 'They look very fit and professional. I'm impressed.'

I wasn't sure what to make of the comment. I knew Tino was just trying to be nice, but had he expected the players to turn up in Hawaiian shirts eating Spam sandwiches? I was just relieved that he hadn't asked why we only had fifteen players on show rather than sixteen.

Our small talk with Tino was interrupted by the news that the Pohnpeian community had arrived with our first day's supply of food for the players. We left Dilshan completing the warm-up and went to offer our heartfelt thanks. Walden was there with his wife Rosa and three other Pohnpeian women. They were carrying boxes from the back of Walden's truck into the changing room. We thanked Walden effusively, but he shrugged us off.

'Hey, it's what Pohnpeians do,' he said. 'We look out for each other. Anyway, we're all really excited to see you guys play.'

I looked into the changing room and saw three containers of food stacked up on a table in the middle of the room. Each one held ten McDonald's takeouts. I don't know why I'd expected anything else. It wasn't exactly what I would have chosen to give a group of sportsmen on the eve of the biggest game of their lives, but beggars couldn't be choosers. I had planned to try to educate the players on sports nutrition during the tour, but I wondered how effectively I could do that with McDonald's wrappers still warm in the bin.

Training ended early, partly due to the searing heat of the late afternoon. Guam was much hotter than Pohnpei. It was a dry, powerful heat that made the sauna-like humidity of PICS Field seem almost hospitable. The players looked a little worried by the temperature as they knew we'd be playing our first game at exactly the same time the next day, but they perked up on entering the changing room and seeing the Holy Grail of fast food on the table. Matt and I shrugged and tucked into a leathery burger each. Tino came and sat with us, but politely insisted he'd already eaten. Halfway through the meal, the door to the dormitory swung open and Robert marched in, slamming it hard behind him.

'Sorry I'm late,' he growled before pointing angrily at Tino, who had turned in surprise to view the latecomer. 'Who's this guy?'

As the secretary general of the Guam FA, Tino was our biggest hope of securing funding for the future of Pohnpei football, and we had to impress him. Robert had just rendered that task a world harder. I was seething and Dilshan looked ready to punch Robert. I wouldn't have stopped him. Once Tino left I called Robert into the dormitory for a meeting. He sat on one side of the table with his head bowed, staring intently at his lap as if trying to find crumbs from the meal. Dilshan and I sat down opposite him. Robert was slowly coming to terms with the fact that he might again be reduced to a spectator on a Pohnpei football tour. There were tears in his eyes.

'Do you realise that you've let everyone down?' Dilshan asked. 'Not just Coach and me, but all the other players. When you mess up like this, it ruins our work.'

Robert offered no excuses. He simply waited for his turn to speak and then muttered an apology. It must have been extremely galling to be given a dressing down by two younger men.

'From now on you have to impress us,' I said. 'You know that you might not get to play on this tour, but I want you to convince me that you deserve to.'

Robert looked heartbroken but he pledged to be a model of professionalism for the remainder of the tour. I had certainly never wanted to bring anyone and not play them at all. However, not only had Robert broken team rules and undermined our efforts to impress Tino, he was also the player who had given me most reason for concern tactically. I wasn't at all sure I could trust him and neither was Dilshan.

'I say we sit him on the bench until the last ten minutes of the last game,' Dilshan said.

'We'll see,' I replied.

I considered taking off the lucky charm necklace Robert had given me but decided against it. However angry I was with him, we needed all the luck we could get.

It was the evening before the opening game against Rovers. Matt had asked around to try and gather some more information about the opposition, but we had very little to go on: we knew they were a mid-table side in Guam's Second Division and that they played in yellow. That was it.

The players had retired to their dorm for the night. Alika was in charge of them now, and I could hear Roger singing and Charles hooting with laughter. Marvin had played the same song at least ten times in succession on his phone, but nobody seemed to notice.

I found Matt sitting on the steps outside the dormitory, staring into the distance. The floodlights had been switched off and night was taking over.

'What if we lose 10–0?' he said. 'After all this work, what if we lose 10–0?'

'I don't know.'

Exactly the same thought had been running through my head. We had done everything we could to create the best possible team and had seen great improvements, but we had no way to compare our lads against the standard in Guam. The most common question from people in England was: 'If Pohnpei were an English team, which division would they be in?' It was impossible to answer. Some of our players were amongst the best athletes I had ever seen. A few had been blessed with exceptional natural talent. But, on the other hand, only a year ago a significant proportion of them had never played an organised game of football. When you add the bizarre climatic conditions that Pohnpei's players are used to and their unique mentality, it becomes too complex an equation to solve.

On a very limited budget, Matt and I had booked in to a small hotel just a mile down a dual carriageway from the Guam FA complex. The price and its location next to a massage parlour and close to a row of strip clubs meant the hotel was mainly frequented by Micronesians on business trips looking to make the most from being in the Central Pacific's Sin City. Matt and I probably got less sleep than any other client, but for very different reasons.

We returned in the morning to the GFA to find Dilshan was already leading a training session. The evening before I had written a schedule on the whiteboard.

10.30 – Breakfast

12.00 – Train

13.00 – Eat

15.00 – Team Meeting

16.00 – Beat Rovers

It was only 10.30 a.m. and the players had already eaten breakfast and gone straight to training. It was baking hot. We ran some set-pieces and walked through some game situations and then retreated to the shade. Guam's players were used to these conditions. Tino had told us that games go on through the day from 9 a.m. to 9 p.m., but in Pohnpei we never started training until the hottest part of the day was over.

The Pohnpeian community had delivered a lunch of fried chicken and fried fish with chips. The players bolted it down and we forced them to rest for a short time to let the food digest and make the most of its limited nutritional value. Alika started up his laptop and put on an American-football-based film, packed full of clichés, but it seemed to put the players in the right mood. A crowd had started to gather for the game. A small group of Pohnpeians, including Walden and Rosa and some members of Denson's extended family, were sitting on one side of the pitch. There was even a local news crew. Some Guamanians had turned up, possibly hoping to see a thrashing.

'They don't play soccer on Pohnpei these days,' I heard one middle-aged local say with authority. 'They play baseball and basketball but they never win at those. No Pohnpei team has ever beaten Guam at anything.'

An hour to go until kick-off and we were huddled in a dressing room that had no air conditioning and was starting to resemble a sauna. Charles had brought Joseph's shirt, and hung it next to the Pohnpei flag we'd packed. The tension was incredible. The team talk I'd been rehearsing in my head for weeks was over in an instant. I reminded the players of how hard they had worked, how much a victory would mean to the people of Pohnpei, and then the players were out on the pitch, warming up. Our squad warmed up as a unit, running through a prepared routine, while the opposition belted a ball around the goalmouth. They appeared in dribs and drabs and stared over at us in surprise. I felt a small stab of pride. But although Rovers didn't look like elite athletes, they did look like a reasonable outfit; we were going to have our work cut out to beat them. Matt and I wheeled a cooler full of drinks over to our bench and shook hands with the referee – a jowly but friendly man who tried in vain to make small talk. We were much too nervous for that.

The team was picked. Robert and Bob were on the bench. I handed the twins their yellow substitute bibs. Bob thanked me sarcastically, Robert thanked me earnestly and they both sat down on the metal bench that was uncomfortably hot in the intense sun. It didn't really matter to Matt and me how hot the bench was because neither of us could contemplate sitting in our tense state. We opted instead to pace the sideline.

In front of around fifty people, the most important match in Pohnpeian football for at least a decade kicked off. And we played excellently. The smooth surface didn't seem to be troubling our players. In fact they thrived on it and passed the ball around with ease. Rovers were doing most of the chasing and even after ten minutes it became clear that at least we wouldn't lose 10–0. Rodrigo shot just over the bar and Matthew forced a save from the goalkeeper, prompting Matt to shout so loudly the fourth official backed away from him. It was all going so well until we conceded a freak goal. A Rovers cross came to Roger, who tried to clear it but his half-volley deflected off Dilshan's back and past a stranded Charles: 1–0.

I had pictured myself as a quiet, dignified and sporting manager and always taken against those who weren't, but in reality the pressure took its toll. Every free kick or corner, even every throw-in we conceded was agony. Every decision that went against us seemed like part of a wider conspiracy. All we could do was watch and shout. Before long Matt and I were yelling and swearing like any professional coach. Matt was practically on the pitch on several occasions, he was so determined to rally our troops.

The ball fell to Dilshan. He turned and ran with it. The opposition had identified him as a danger man and sent three towards him, but he'd already looped a through ball for Rodrigo, who had emitted his trademark grunt. Rodrigo ran on to the ball, getting there before the defender, and thumped it past the goalkeeper for the equaliser. There was mayhem on the bench. Rodrigo looked quietly thrilled as Dilshan and Marvin jumped on his back in delight. I turned round and noticed that even Bob and Robert were grinning.

But things didn't quite go our way. Just before half-time there was finally a lapse in concentration and Rovers took full advantage with a low shot making it 2–1. The second half proved little better. We thought Dilshan was about to level with twenty minutes of the game left but his shot hit the post and rolled agonisingly along the line before being booted to safety.

Nothing seemed to be going right and the game was effectively ended when the referee gave a penalty to Rovers for a foul by Mike. It was a clear-cut foul, and well inside the box, but Matt and I both howled our frustration, not at the decision but at the way the game had turned out. Charles dived heroically and nearly saved the spot-kick but it crossed the line for 3–1.

Dilshan was fuming. He began to put in some late tackles and tangle with the opposition players. He chased down a through ball but was never going to get there before the goalkeeper. As the keeper gathered the ball, Dilshan thumped into him. In England he would have been sent off for that kind of tackle. Luckily the referee was in a lenient mood, but our captain had to come off before he offended again. We sent Bob on as a third striker. He was full of energy and enthusiasm, but that worked to his detriment as, to my chagrin, he committed two terrible lungeing tackles and was caught offside three times in ten minutes. In the dying moments Tom went forward for a corner and took advantage of his stature to rise above the defenders and head home for 3–2. We frantically sent every player forward in search of an equaliser, but there was no time. We had lost.

In the aftermath of a defeat, especially one that could so easily have been a victory, there's no measured reaction: just raw emotion. We hadn't lost 10–0 and we'd given a good account of ourselves, but it was a crushing blow. We gathered for a team talk.

'I know that you're feeling upset at the moment, but I'm proud of the way you played. If we do that in our next game, we will win,' I said. 'I want you to remember how this feels because then it'll be even sweeter tomorrow.'

But there was nothing anyone could say to ease the devastation. Dilshan insisted on apologising to the team for 'playing like shit', though he was drowned out by others maintaining they had played worse. Ryan was staring into space. Denson was in tears, covering his face with his blue and white bandanna.

'It would've meant so much to win,' he said. 'My family is here and I wanted this so bad.'

Rocky was just furious. Without a direction for his anger he paced aimlessly around the car park, refusing to talk to anyone. He was still walking laps two hours later before he relented and came in for food. Only Rodrigo looked happy. He had scored our first goal and, try as he might, he couldn't keep a small smile off his face.

'We thought you were fantastic,' Rosa said as we left the pitch.

'That was even better than we thought. You guys can really play. They should be proud, not upset,' Walden grinned.

Tino had been watching and was also full of praise for the team, but we didn't want to hear it. What really mattered was that we had another game the next day, against the Crushers. Furthermore, Tino told us that the president of the Guam FA, Richard Lai, would be turning up to watch. There was no time to mope and feel sorry for ourselves. We needed to win a game on this tour and that was unlikely to happen against a Guam national team, even if they picked an Under-19 side. We hadn't come to Guam to lose three matches in a row. I hadn't come this far to slink back to England with my tail between my legs. We had to beat the Crushers.

10

CRUSHED

Everyone had an explanation for why we had lost to Rovers. Some blamed the weather, some the pitch, some the referee, but we were able to silence the arguments by producing a DVD of the game in full. There was a risk that we might end up demoralising the team further by showing them footage of the defeat, but while it was painful viewing it seemed to galvanise morale. They had never seen video of themselves playing competitively before, so the players sat transfixed as images of the previous day's game played on the computer. There were howls of laughter as Charles appeared, adjusting his shorts. A collective wince accompanied the own goal that put us behind while a massive cheer followed Rodrigo's goal. Charles slapped Rodrigo on the back hard, nearly knocking the smiling winger off his chair. After the video, the players took it in turns to suggest what needed improving and what had gone well. The mood was upbeat and everyone wanted kick-off time to arrive and give us a chance to redeem ourselves.

Again we conducted a light training session in the late morning. The players were more focused than ever before. Nobody kicked balls aimlessly at the goal between drills this time, and there was a lot less light-hearted chat. Towards the end of training we ran a simple shooting drill, allowing players to find the net with Charles in goal to make a few confidence-building saves. The fourth shot was struck powerfully by Denson to Charles's left side. It was always going in and everyone expected Charles to leave it to its natural course. But he was having none of it and hurled himself sideways, getting a hand to it but failing to prevent the ball nestling in the corner. As he pushed himself back up to his feet it was clear that something wasn't right.

'It's my wrist,' he said through gritted teeth. 'It's not good.'

Over the course of the day it became clear that Charles's wrist was really getting to him, but he tried to pretend it was all right for fear of not being able to play. Away from Charles's view Alika had pulled on a pair of goalkeeper's gloves for the first time in half a year and Dilshan was hitting some routine shots at him. Alika was sweating profusely and considerably overweight, but his natural ability was clear. He looked reassuringly sharp and was catching the ball cleanly despite the arthritis that caused him some discomfort. And suddenly Brian Taylor was there. Brian had been discharged from hospital earlier that day after doctors in Guam confirmed he had suffered a minor concussion and a significant allergic reaction to the drugs he had been given in Pohnpei. He had immediately taken a taxi to the Guam FA facility. Except for a telltale black eye and a cut on his cheek, Brian looked perfectly healthy – but there was no way we could let him play. Despite his protests, I told him firmly that until he could get a doctor's note saying he was fit to play he wouldn't set foot on the pitch.

'I'll work on that,' he said thoughtfully. 'But I'm staying for the game to cheer us on.'

It was slightly less hot than it had been the day before. News of yesterday's game had spread and a larger group had gathered to watch. We gathered in the dressing room for the team talk. Charles was kitted up and ready to go. He declared that he was 100 per cent fit.

There was no holding back. It was time for stirring words.

'You never know how many chances you get in your life to represent your country. Make the most of this one. Yesterday you played the best game of your lives and you lost. Today if you do the same, you will win. For Pohnpei!'

After Matt, Dilshan and I had successfully whipped the team up into a state of manic excitement, Dilshan led a chant of Pohnpei! Pohnpei! Pohnpei!' The players filed towards the door still chanting and stamping their boots on the floor in time. Wearing bright orange, the Crushers were on the field and had heard our entrance. They turned to watch as the blue and white shirts burst out of the dressing room and began their warm-up. Walden gave us a thumbs-up and a few spectators continued the chant: 'Pohnpei! Pohnpei! Pohnpei!'

Robert and Bob were again handed their bibs and we returned to the sideline. I looked across the field and saw Tino sitting with a couple of people I didn't recognise. I guessed that one was Richard Lai, Guam's Football Association president and the East Asia Football Association finance officer – the man we had to impress above everyone else. Just before kick-off, Denson, Dilshan and Mike rushed off for the customary pre-game urination. When they returned Mike had changed his shirt. The back now read '9 J. Welson'. Charles slapped him on the back.

For our opposition, this was a friendly game, but for us it was the most important match we had ever played. The pride of an island was at stake. Our intensity shocked the Crushers. Every time they had the ball a player would be on top of them. Marvin terrorised their left back while Mike ran rings round their chubby right back. Roger, whom I had so often reprimanded in Pohnpei for not taking things seriously enough, was all business. He was winning every header and putting in some crunching but entirely fair challenges.

The breakthrough didn't take long to come. Ryan won the ball just inside the Crushers half and flicked it through to Matthew, who buried it without a second's thought. The celebrations were muted this time. We weren't going to get carried away. But our lead was soon doubled when Dilshan found Ryan, who held off a defender and slotted the ball past a goalkeeper who seemed more interested in shouting at his defence than diving.

Dilshan and Nick were dominating the midfield. In the first game Dilshan had looked slightly daunted by the weight of expectations on him, but this time he was running the game effortlessly. While Dilshan was doing the grafting, Nick was getting a rare chance to show his attacking strength. On his first major foray forward Nick picked the ball up on the edge of the box and calmly struck it into the roof of the net: 3–0.

Despite the scoreline, the players remained focused. Each goal was marked with a high-five or two before Dilshan would call for concentration and they would settle back into positions. The Crushers managed a few shots, but Charles was ready for them. He gingerly held his wrist after each save but stopped immediately if he saw we were watching.

Matthew had a second just before half-time when he completed a carbon copy of the first. We reached the break 4–0 ahead. The Crushers looked like they wanted to go home and had started to yell at each other.

Despite our overwhelming advantage, Matt and I took nothing

for granted. The players were grinning and laughing. We soon put a stop to that.

'We've done nothing yet,' I told them. 'Go out and play like it's the start of the game again.'

The second half started and the Crushers looked a better side. Rocky had to make a superb sliding tackle to prevent a shooting chance, while Denson repelled cross after cross, shrugging off strikers with ease. It was all getting too much for Robert to bear. He was itching to get on the field. Unsolicited, he started to warm up and then began to bounce a ball against the back of the bench. He was so full of restless energy that he began to kick at a nearby bin. The metallic clink was drowned out by Brian bellowing encouragement to the players in his distinctive Californian accent.

Marvin passed to Mike and Mike smashed the ball home for 5–0. Ryan made it 6–0 and the Pohnpeians on the sideline couldn't believe what was going on. Every time a Pohnpei player got the ball there was a cheer. The charismatic Roger, lining up just metres from the Pohnpeian fans, had attracted a following and a chant of 'Go Roger! Go Roger!' started every time he got the ball.

It was almost physically impossible for us to throw away this lead, but there was no way I could relax. I'd spent my whole football life seeing teams I loved throw it all away.

Bob came on to replace Matthew, but Ryan was also clearly exhausted. With such a tight schedule of games we needed to rest him but would have to reshuffle.

'Let's put Tom up front,' Matt said.

I'd never seen Tom play up front. But there was very little to be lost. This way we could also finally unleash Robert. At 6–0 up with fifteen minutes left, it was time he got on the pitch. Robert entered the action like a wild dog, snapping at the heels of the Crushers and getting caught horribly out of position on several occasions. Luckily, Denson was on hand to clear up.

Tom had the manoeuvrability of an aircraft carrier but his ball control made up for it. He happily shrugged off two or three defenders each time he got the ball and was rarely dispossessed. Dilshan laid it off to Tom and the giant defender-turned-striker toe-poked it from the edge of the box into the corner of the net: 7–0.

The Crushers did get on the score sheet, beating Charles with a well-placed drive from twenty yards.

'Nice shot!' Charles yelled as he picked the ball out of the net.

Denson was not so happy.

'What the hell do you mean, "nice shot"?' he snapped at Charles and shook his head.

Charles was in some pain. We beckoned at him and Alika ran on to the field and out of retirement. The remainder of the game was quiet, but Alika made two good stops and dealt with crosses as if he had never been away.

The final whistle sounded. We had done it. This was the one eventuality I hadn't prepared for. I suppose I could have gone wild, and led a one-man conga line around Guam chanting '7–1! 7–1!' Instead I stood there arms folded with a smile spreading across my face as I watched my players.

Rosa and Walden led a pitch invasion of ten or so Pohnpei fans as the players hugged each other. Denson punched the air triumphantly. Rocky was running around manically with the flag.

'We got one!' Dilshan yelled. 'We got one!'

We all shook hands but decided that didn't do justice to the situation and opted for manly bear hugs. Charles and Mike walked along the pitch, arms around each other like an old married couple.

I don't know whether any words passed between them but the elation was clear.

A baffled Crushers player walked over to offer his congratulations. He was the oldest and probably the captain.

'Well played,' he said. 'We didn't really think it would be such a serious game. I didn't even know Pohnpei had a team.'

I looked over to the stands but Tino and the mysterious man sitting next to him had gone.

The next day was a much-needed day off for the players, but not for the coaches. We had received a phone call from Tino, who congratulated us on our win over the Crushers and told us that Richard Lai wanted to meet us. He gave us an address and a time. The address turned out to be Shirley's Restaurant – a slightly dilapidated fast-food eatery. The Guam Football Association car was parked outside, so we knew it was the right place. Tino was waiting for us inside at a table on his own.

'That was some game yesterday!' he said. 'Your boys can really play. The football was excellent.'

Richard had seen most of the game but had been called away towards the end. He was on his way to meet us because he believed he could help Micronesia get FIFA funding. When he arrived, he wasn't what I was expecting. From across a football field I hadn't been able to see that he was a short man with Chinese features, and when he spoke it became clear that English wasn't his first language.

'I believe that Micronesia can have football,' he said. 'But you need to understand that it is about more than what you do on the pitch. You need committees, registered players and teams, by-laws and constitutions.

'We helped the Northern Mariana Islands and now they're doing great,' Richard continued. 'We would also be happy to help you, but you need to have a strong organisation with a good secretary general and a good president. Do you have that?'

I thought of Clark Graham, who had been full of enthusiasm when we were in a meeting in Pohnpei but hadn't been in touch since. Only Dilshan could really represent Micronesia, but he was too young to be taken seriously by middle-aged men in suits.

'I think you're maybe strong enough to play in the annual Marianas Cup against Guam and Northern Mariana Islands,' Richard said. 'Have someone get in touch with me and we'll see about that. Anyway, I have to go now.'

And within fifteen minutes, Richard had come and gone. He'd made some exciting promises, but left much more dangling tantalisingly out of our reach. After this tour it would be Dilshan's responsibility, but it was a great deal of pressure to put on one young man.

For now, though, we had more immediate problems to deal with: namely, a grand finale in the shape of a game against a Guam national team. The last time a full Guam national side played Pohnpei was a decade ago and the result had been 16–1. And it was terrifying to think how far Guam had come as a footballing nation in the intervening ten years. They had gone from complete obscurity to respectability and were one of the fastest-climbing nations in the FIFA World Rankings. While we could console ourselves with the thought that this team would probably comprise mostly Under-19 players, even their Under-19 side had a professional coach and players who had been playing since the age of five.

Crushed

It was tough to get my players back down to earth after the win over the Crushers. They had spent their second day off at a water park under the watchful eye of Alika. It had been a day of ogling women in bikinis and eating junk food but strictly no alcohol was allowed and Dilshan had firmly reinforced that rule. Now we were asking for one last big effort on the pitch and hoping that the drama so far hadn't taken too great a toll.

The big day had arrived – Pohnpei v. Guam. Even though we were likely to be taking on a youth team and had come to realise that simply taking part in the match was a victory in itself, that didn't reduce the tension. After all, this was the climax of a chain of events that had been set in motion way back in November 2007. So many trials and tribulations and ups and downs had followed and all for this moment – we were leading Pohnpei into what was to all intents and purposes an international fixture.

Damage limitation is a negative phrase and one that a coach can never use in front of his team, but away from the players Matt and I were able to admit that keeping the score down against Guam was probably our most realistic aim. We didn't intend to play a different system as that would invite pressure, but we were going to encourage Nick to protect the defence more than he had in the last game, and if there were opportunities for quick breaks we had to take them. There was a sickly, oppressive heat and dark clouds gathered overhead. Rain would be most welcome, I thought. We knew how to play in the rain.

We hadn't been told which Guam national side we'd be facing. They had turned up early and were already on the pitch training when we gathered for our team talk. To my relief it seemed that it was an Under-19 side with a couple of slightly older-looking players tagged on.

I felt that this game merited a more formal approach and opted to wear a black shirt with a collar in honour of the occasion. Matt had stuck to his Hawaiian shirt policy. We wrapped up our pre-game formalities and the teams lined up. Guam had six substitutes and their coach sat calmly on the bench, barking the occasional order at his charges. We had Bob, Robert and Brian, who had produced a (probably fake) note from his doctor saying that he could play if necessary. Alika was also sitting on the bench but had indicated that he really wasn't fit for this one. He was still hurting from his unexpected return from retirement. Charles had the gloves on.

The difference in quality between the Guam side and the previous day's Crushers was immediately apparent. They passed quickly, moved quickly and left our players largely chasing shadows for the first five minutes. But we were holding our own for the first quarter of the game. At the ten-minute mark I calculated that even if we conceded every five minutes from here on it would only be 16–0.

The sky was now getting dark and a few spots of rain fell. Matt and I were shouting ourselves hoarse, partly to try and remind players of things we had practised but mostly just to vent our own nervous energy.

Guam went ahead. It was a lethal strike from the edge of the eighteen-yard box and came completely out of the blue. And soon after, equally without warning, it was 2–0. There seemed to be no danger as two Guam players exchanged passes twenty-five yards from goal, but then a striker who looked about twelve curled the ball neatly past Charles. We were having lots of the ball now and Dilshan was playing excellently, but there was no final product. When we did get shooting chances they were weak shots, straight at the goalkeeper.

Despite being behind, the players were starting to show more confidence and were even getting the better of the 50–50 challenges. The passing was smooth and crisp and Marvin swung over a series of brilliant crosses. Matthew was bullying their centre-back, who kept complaining to the referee, and Dilshan kept making mazy runs. But then Charles got injured. He'd come sliding out to scoop up the ball and landed on his bad wrist. He didn't look happy and for the first time wasn't insistent that he could play on. We were in trouble. I turned to look at Alika, who shook his head.

'Let me go on.'

Brian had his goalkeeper's jersey on. I looked at Matt. He looked at me. Brian looked pleadingly at us both. The referee whistled to signal that a decision had to be made – Charles had to play on or be replaced. The choice was a grim one – call Denson back between the posts for the first time since he'd lived in Guam, and in the process lose a crucial main defender, or allow Brian to play, knowing that if he were to get another blow to the head it could be very serious. Brian ran on and I let him. I turned and saw that Matt, like me, had clenched his hands in silent prayer.

The third goal was a hammer blow, scored on the break during our most promising spell of possession. Brian had no chance. He dived acrobatically but the shot was beyond his reach. At half-time we were 3–0 down but had played better than ever before.

During the fifteen-minute break, the heavens finally opened. The rain was torrential. By the start of the second half it was hard to see your hand in front of your face, let alone what was going on in the game. Guam's coach settled back in his dugout but Matt and I continued to walk the sideline, soaked to the skin. My shirt was sticking to me and I started to shiver but all we cared about was what was happening in front of us. As I had hoped, the rain had tipped things in our favour. The slippery conditions suited us and Nick had two decent shots that their keeper had to be alert to. Dilshan got through one-on-one with the goalkeeper but almost had too much time and shot into his stomach. It was all Pohnpei now. The Guam players looked like they wanted a warm shower, but our boys were playing the last twenty minutes of their first and possibly last ever tour.

Roger carried the ball forward and played a pass towards Matthew and then suddenly it was pitch black. The lights had gone out. Drenched, but still full of adrenaline, Matt called the players over into a huddle and I told Dilshan to keep them warm, so we would be ready when the lights came on. But the lights didn't come back on. An embarrassed Guam FA official came over to the bench and told us that it would take at least two hours to get the lights working again. Guam's coach had accepted the abandonment and the Guam official offered an apology but hoped we would accept the score too.

A day before, we probably would have shaken on a 3–0 defeat, but not now. I knew it was over, but couldn't hold back a torrent of anger. Matt had to take me to one side to calm me down.

'It's over, mate,' Matt said. 'Typical Guam, bunch of amateurs! I knew we should have played it at PICS.'

We both laughed.

There was nothing to be gained now from letting rip. Instead we shook hands with our soggy and confused players and explained the situation.

Tino came over and apologised for the floodlights.

'We've got something special as a send-off, though,' he said. 'Come and see.'

We led the Pohnpei team up the stairs of the clubhouse. The Pohnpeians from the crowd were there along with some Guam FA staff, Tino and a photographer. Stacked up against a Guam Football Association banner were boxes of boots and bags of footballs.

'This is a small donation from the Guam Football Association,' Tino said, shaking my hand for the photo. 'There's lots more and we hope to be able to make an annual donation. Make sure you come back again next year.'

It was a great gesture, but the timing was odd. Just a few minutes ago Guam had been our opponents – the team we had trained for so long to fight. Suddenly, without warning we had been jolted into remembering that they were actually our only allies in the football world.

The rain had stopped. Photos were taken and slowly the players started to come to terms with the fact the tour was over. Rocky was one of the last to shrug off the abandonment of the match. He insisted that the game should be replayed the next day. He only changed his mind when Dilshan pointed out that playing tomorrow would prevent them going on a massive end-of-tour bender.

The players were free to do as they pleased. We'd kept them cooped up in the Guam FA facility for their entire stay, but now they were no longer footballers but just young men celebrating an amazing achievement. Matt and I had always planned to join the party on the final night, but were hit by overwhelming exhaustion.

The highs and lows of the last few weeks and months suddenly took their toll, and we had a pretty quiet night as we tried to contemplate the future, and life without Pohnpei.

We had no real idea where we would go from here but we had done all we could do in Pohnpei short of moving there permanently. The future of the game on the island depended on locals taking charge, otherwise it would always have a temporary feel. Now it was up to Dilshan and the likes of Rocky, Marvin, Nick and even Bob and Robert to go home and become the next generation of leaders.

The players had a wide range of destinations for the evening. Some went on a tour of Guam's exotic-dancing circuit and others hit the casinos. Marvin, Roger, Ryan and Rodrigo stayed at the Guam Football Association facility and watched a couple of films.

The next day there were some pained faces at the airport. Rocky was hugging everyone, laughing as they recoiled from the pungent scent of alcohol he exuded. Charles ran off to the toilets and returned looking green. Dilshan had sunglasses on, which he refused to remove. Robert was still drunk. In the departure lounge, Rocky fell asleep draped in the Pohnpei flag. Matt jogged my arm.

'Look, it's Churchill,' he said.

Churchill Edward, the lieutenant governor of Pohnpei, was about to board the same flight as us. He must have seen us before – we were hardly a group you could miss. He made eye contact with Matt and felt compelled to come over.

'Just been on business for a few days,' he said with a smile. 'I heard you guys got a win. I was very impressed.'

It dawned on me that Churchill had been in Guam during our games but hadn't shown up. No wonder he was avoiding us. I stopped myself asking him whether there had been any progress with fixing the lights at PICS Field. These weren't my battles any more.

I'd love to say we were met at Pohnpei Airport by hordes of screaming fans. We weren't: we were greeted by the same small group of people who had seen us off. But as we travelled round Kolonia it became clear that the island had taken notice of what had happened in Guam. The island grapevine had spread news of the win against the Crushers long before we got home. The players were being treated differently – they were being shown a level of respect they weren't accustomed to. Everyone wanted to talk to them and to hear their stories from Guam and every politician wanted to take credit for their long-standing support of football.

On the journey home I'd had time to reflect on what had been achieved. In little over eighteen months we had transformed football in Pohnpei from a series of sporadic, poorly attended kick-arounds to an organised sport for some of the island's most gifted athletes. On leaving for Guam I had secretly feared that we might not even score a single goal in our three games. We had done much more than that: we had won a game and won it convincingly. Furthermore we had impressed Guam's FA with our conduct on and off the field and built working relationships that could take the game on to the next level. Not bad going for a couple of Sunday League nobodies.

There was more good news waiting for us from Jim Tobin – the man who had always supported football. He'd applied for an International Olympic Committee grant to provide a salary for a football coach to deliver workshops on each of the Micronesian islands. A while ago we'd discussed the grant and suggested that Dilshan's name should be put forward, and now he was to become Micronesia's first professional football coach.

Matt and I were delighted for Dilshan, but this confirmed that we could never get assistance to return to Pohnpei. The Olympic Committee grants that had funded accommodation and occasionally flights would now provide Dilshan's salary. It was time for us to move on. We were already part of Pohnpei's football history. Dilshan had taken the reins – the future of Micronesian football was in his hands.

EXTRA TIME

Dilshan is already out there. He's counting his paces under his breath, dropping a cone every ten. He finishes marking out a square on a newly mown PICS Field and lightly kicks a tuft of cut grass off the pitch. A car horn sounds and he looks up with a smile.

Denson's taxi has arrived. The passenger doors open and Nick, Roger and Tom jump out. Ryan pulls up next to them in his shiny Toyota with Matthew sitting alongside him.

As the newcomers lace up their boots, they notice Marvin in full football kit sitting in the stand opposite with his wife and a young baby in his arms.

'Where's Rocky?' Charles calls to Dilshan.

Dilshan nods towards the running track, where Rocky is completing his fifth lap, impatient to get started.

'What's this, island time?' he shouts.

The training session starts and a small crowd gathers just to sit and watch. Every time the ball goes off the field a small child runs from the stands to kick it back. It becomes a competition to see who can get there first.

Dilshan sets up a shooting drill. Mike rifles the ball into the net, drawing applause from the gathered spectators. Bob fires well wide – Robert howls with delight.

Dilshan lays the ball off to Roger, who flicks it up and attempts an acrobatic volley. The ball flies over Charles, over the goal and on to the running track where it is trapped first time by an onlooker.

'Joseph, kick it back,' Charles yells.

The heavens open.

ACKNOWLEDGEMENTS

Up Pohnpei is not written as a historical text or an anthropological study on Micronesia. For those interested in further research on the region I would strongly recommend contacting Micronesian Seminar, who have an excellent website and a huge library.

I would like to thank the following people, without whom this book could never have been written:

UK

- Matthew Conrad, the only person I could have embarked on this journey with.
- Charles Musana, who sowed the seeds of football in Pohnpei.
- Larry Coyne, who saved the day by making the tour of Guam possible.
- My family, for their support, and in particular Mark for his guidance and willingness to risk his reputation by hosting a hastily assembled fundraiser.
- Lizzie's parents William and Alex, for their generosity and advice, and all of the Howard family who championed my cause including Miranda, who built us a website when she had a million other things to do.

- My agent Jamie Coleman, for his infinite patience and passion for all things Pohnpei. Also Samar Hammam and everyone else at Toby Eady Associates.
- My editor Lisa Owens, who believed in the book from the very beginning and was a pleasure to work with, and everyone at Profile Books.
- The Conrad family, especially Jeremy Conrad, Pohnpeian football's number one fan.
- Chris Sweet and all at Sherborne Town and Yeovil Town.
- Corry Shaw, for organising our fundraiser, and all who took part in it.
- Steve Menary, who set me straight on non–FIFA football.
- Rachel Howe, for being a lovely, understanding flatmate.
- Everyone who sponsored a player, bought a shirt, attended our shambolic fundraiser or gave a Pound for Pohnpei.

Pohnpei

- My players.
- Jim Tobin, for believing football could succeed in Micronesia. Also, Lestly Ashby and everyone else at the FSM NOC.
- Dilshan, the Senarathgodas and the Masilamonys, who were my family in Pohnpei.
- George Steven and Michaela Corr, whose dedication to Micronesian athletics was an inspiration.
- Walden Weilbacher, for helping Joseph and his family and making us at home in Guam, as well as Rosa Weilbacher and the Pohnpeian community in Guam.
- Albert Carlot, Emi and Steve Gatting, Simon Ellis, Damian Richard, Steve Finnen, Jason Cuite, Bill Jaynes, Phillip

Acknowledgements

Prouhet, Rosie at the Continental Micronesia desk in Pohnpei Airport.

- Tino San Gil, Richard Lai and all the staff at the Guam FA.
- Bob McGrath, a great supporter of sport on Pohnpei who will be sadly missed.

And, most importantly, I would like to thank Lizzie, who was with me every step of the way and never let me give up.